What the Bible Teaches Al

Marriage, Divorce & Remarriage

by David E. Sproule, II

ISBN-10: 1494220407
ISBN-13: 978-1494220402

Introduction

This material was written, compiled and used for a Bible Class at the Palm Beach Lakes church of Christ in 2013. It was written in outline form to simplify the content, the formatting and the application for a Bible Class setting. Due to time constraints, the study was not as exhaustive as it could (or should) have been.

The subject of Marriage, Divorce and Remarriage is a vast topic with numerous aspects and issues that require great time and deliberation to thoroughly examine. While limited somewhat in its scope, it is believed that the following pages will provide a basic introduction to the fundamental principles needed to grasp, explain, teach and defend this vitally important topic.

Each chapter lists bibliographical information to aid in further study. (At the end of Chapter 8, a supplementary list of sources is provided beyond the ones consulted for this study.) It is hoped that additional chapters and studies will be added to this book in future years.

Table of Contents

Chapter 1: <u>Introductory Matters</u>

I. **Having a Biblical understanding of this subject (MDR) is of critical importance! (Not trivial!)**
    A. First of all, it is a matter of eternal significance!
        1. This earthly relationship issue directly affects our relationship with God!
        2. And, our relationship with God determines whether we go to heaven or not!
    B. This matter has a national significance!
        1. Marriage and the family are the foundation of a nation's health (ours is crumbling).
        2. The marriage relationship, as defined by God, has been on a steep decline in the U.S.
            (a) Our nation has left the laws and morality of God for their own subjective morality.
            (b) The rise of the divorce rate, the prevalence of multiple marriages, the rejection of marriage in general and the promotion of homosexuality have destroyed marriage.
    C. This matter has a church significance!
        1. The church and its members have not been immune to this issue.
        2. Even Christians are divorcing and remarrying at alarming rates (for various reasons).
        3. Some Christians have left the laws & morality of God for their own subjective morality.
        4. Evangelistic efforts are impacted by the previous marriages of prospects.
        5. Brethren often disagree on this issue, leading to controversy within the church, and triggering some Christians to "preacher-shop" for one who will validate their marriage.
        6. Shepherds are placed in difficult positions, requiring tough (unpopular) decisions.
    D. This matter has a Biblical significance!
        1. Marriage and the home are the first and oldest institution known to man (Gen. 2).
        2. Biblical precepts outline God's will for the marriage relationship and must be obeyed.

II. **Studying and teaching this subject (MDR) is a very sensitive matter!**
    A. This subject reaches out and touches everyone – personally, emotionally & with family.
    B. Self-justification and justification of loved ones, at any cost, often takes precedence.
    C. When there are children involved, the matter is complicated exponentially.
    D. The highly controversial nature of this subject has divided congregations and families.
    E. Discerning and abiding by God's law is often set aside for one's personal preferences.

III. **Studying marriage, divorce and remarriage must be entered with the proper attitude!**
    A. Proper study must include a proper attitude toward marriage itself!
        1. Marriage is not unnecessary, a tradition of the past or a product of culture.
        2. Marriage was the first institution created by God, and must be respected as such.
    B. Proper study must include a proper attitude toward God Himself!
        1. Our love for God must exceed our love for anyone else.
            (a) Luke 10:27; 14:26 – Love God supremely, letting nothing impede that love.
        2. Our submission to God must override our submission to anyone else.
            (a) John 6:38-40; 8:29; Col. 1:10; 2 Tim. 2:4; 3:4; Heb. 10:7; Luke 22:42
        3. Our attitude of love and submission should lead us to true repentance from sin.
            (a) Matt. 3:8; 2 Cor. 7:9-10; Acts 26:20; Rom. 2:4
        4. Our respect for God will not allow us to improperly invoke His love and mercy as justification for sinful actions (Rom. 6:1, 15; 3:8; Psa. 25:10; 69:13; 85:10).

C. Proper study must include a proper attitude toward God's Word!
   1. A proper attitude respects the perfection of God's revelation, knowing it is complete.
      (a) 2 Tim. 3:16-17; 2 Pet. 1:21; Jas. 1:25; 2 Pet. 1:3; Jude 3
   2. A proper attitude objectively seeks the truth without preconceived ideas.
      (a) Prov. 14:12; Phil. 3:7; John 7:17; Matt. 5:6; 2 Thess. 2:10
   3. A proper attitude recognizes that the Bible is knowable and understandable.
      (a) John 8:32; 17:17; Eph. 3:4; 5:17; Matt. 22:23-29; 2 Tim. 2:15; 1 John 2:21
   4. A proper attitude desires to obey God's truth regardless of cost or where it leads.
      (a) Rom. 12:1; John 6:67-68; Matt. 8:19-22; Luke 9:23-26; 2 Tim. 3:12; Rom. 6:7-19
   5. A proper attitude accepts that some consequences to sin are unalterable (Gal. 6:7).
D. Proper study must include a proper attitude toward one another!
   1. A proper attitude possesses and demonstrates agape love for all.
      (a) Col. 3:12-14; Mt. 5:43-48; John 13:34-35; 1 Cor. 16:14; Rom. 12:10; 1 Cor. 13:4-7
   2. A proper attitude is gracious and forgiving but not compromising.
      (a) Jas. 4:4; Eph. 4:32; John 17:17; Gal. 2:5; 4:16

IV. **Studying marriage, divorce and remarriage must be entered with the proper authority!**
   A. When it comes to marriage, divorce and remarriage, which standard shall we use?
   B. Proper Authority Option #1: Fickle Emotions
      1. Our emotions sometimes prevail when something doesn't seem fair or right.
         (a) "These aren't fair": Ezra 10:10-11; Josh. 7:24-26; Matt. 19:16-22
         (b) Actually, these things are fair and right because God said so!
      2. Our emotions sometimes prevail when something doesn't make sense.
         (a) "These don't make sense": 2 Kgs. 5:10-14; Num. 21:14-19; Josh. 6:1-7; John 9:6-7
         (b) Actually, the only sense they needed to make was God commanded it to be done.
      3. Our emotions are not qualified to be the authority!
         (a) Jer. 10:23; Isa. 55:8-9; Prov. 16:25; 3:5-6; Rom. 11:34
         (b) We are not qualified to question or doubt God or His standard. Just believe & do!
      4. Our emotions do not determine or change Biblical teaching!
   C. Proper Authority Option #2: Family Situations
      1. To avoid condemning family, some seek to justify their situation, creating a "new standard."
      2. However, the Bible "says what it means" and it "means what it says"!
      3. What if a family member is never baptized? Or becomes a homosexual? Standard?
      4. If one family situation can be used to prove God's approval, then any family situation could be used to prove God's approval, which means no situation would ever be wrong.
      5. Our families and their marriages do not determine or change Biblical teaching!
   D. Proper Authority Option #3: Fellow Brethren
      1. Some try to find a preacher who agrees with them and approves of their marriage.
      2. Some may argue that more brethren agree with them & their marriage than do not.
      3. How could fellow human beings ever be considered as a proper authority?
         (a) Ex. 23:2; Matt. 7:13-14; John 12:42-43; 2 Cor. 5:9; 10:12; Prov. 14:12; 1 John 4:1
      4. Our brethren do not determine or change Biblical teaching!
   E. Proper Authority Option #4: Flawless Word of God (which is actually the only "option"!)
      1. The Word of God is the only standard that is objective, Divine and pleasing to God.
      2. The Word of God is the sole authority for all religious matters (Mt. 28:18; Col. 3:17).
      3. The Word of God is the final authority that will judge us (John 12:48; 2 Cor. 5:10).

V. Studying marriage, divorce and remarriage must be entered with the proper analysis!
   A. Proper analysis requires:
      1. "Handling aright the word of truth" (2 Tim. 2:15).
      2. Love for truth and desire to know it (2 Thess. 2:10; John 7:17; Matt. 5:6).
      3. Humility and an open mind (Jer. 9:23-24; Jas. 4:7-10; Isa. 66:2; Prov. 23:23).
      4. A willingness to apply what is learned (Jas. 1:22-25; Matt. 7:21-27).
      5. Studying the content of each passage (defining words, observing grammar, etc.).
      6. Studying the context of each passage (the immediate, the book, the entire Bible).
      7. Gathering all the relevant Scriptural evidence, the sum of God's Word (Psa. 119:160).
      8. Handling the evidence correctly (seeking its original meaning with sound hermeneutics).
      9. Refusing to add to or take away from what is revealed (Rev. 22:18-19; Deut. 12:32).
      10. Staying within the truth, observing it carefully and completely (1 Cor. 4:6; Jn. 8:31).
   B. After proper analysis, hold only to that which is true (1 Th. 5:21; Acts 17:11; 2 Tim. 1:13).

VI. Keys to remember when studying the Bible's teaching on marriage, divorce & remarriage:
   A. Marriage is sacred (Heb. 13:4).
   B. As marriage was created by God, He alone has the right to regulate it (Gen. 2:24; Mt. 19:6).
   C. God's Word is our only standard; it must be taught, respected and obeyed (Matt. 7:21).
   D. The Bible's teaching about MDR is not complicated, cloaked or contradictory.
   E. Actually, the Bible's teaching about MDR is straightforward, simple and systematic.
   F. Do what it says about marriage and you'll have no problems.

VII. There are numerous and varying positions on marriage, divorce and remarriage today:
   A. Marriage is merely a cultural development which has evolved over the years.
   B. Living together, without and/or before being married, is acceptable and advisable.
   C. Having an open marriage (mutual agreement to have sex outside of marriage) is healthy.
   D. Homosexual marriages are equally as legitimate as heterosexual marriages.
   E. The practice of polygamy (having multiple spouses) is Biblically authorized & approved.
   F. God's marriage laws are not amenable to non-Christians.
   G. God's marriage laws in Matthew 19:9 are not part of N.T. & not applicable to Christians.
   H. God's marriage laws in Matthew 19:9 apply only to Christians, as a "covenant passage."
   I. Divorce and remarriage is permitted for any cause.
   J. Divorce and remarriage is not permitted for any cause.
   K. Whatever marriage or divorce the civil law permits is acceptable to God.
   L. Everyone has a right to be married.
   M. Death is the only cause for remarriage.
   N. Baptism washes away all divorces/remarriages and absolves all adulterous relationships.
   O. A person may abide in whatever marital relationship he finds himself when he's baptized, as Christianity has sanctified that relationship.
   P. Repentance only requires one to be sorry and to promise to never do it again.
   Q. Adultery means only "covenant breaking" (not actually any sexual activity), after which one can pray, ask forgiveness and remarry.
   R. A Christian may remarry if his/her non-Christian spouse departs and leaves him/her.
   S. Divorce and remarriage is permitted for viewing pornography.
   T. A spouse guilty of fornication (and put away for it) may remarry.
   U. Divorce and remarriage is only permitted for the innocent spouse who puts away his/her mate for fornication.

BIBLIOGRAPHY
For Chapter 1

Baird, James O. *And I Say Unto You.* Oklahoma City: B&B Bookhouse, 1981.

Edwards, Earl. "Exegesis of Matthew 19:3-12." *Building Stronger Christian Families (1992 Freed-Hardeman University Lectureship).* Ed. Winford Claiborne. Henderson, TN: Freed-Hardeman University, 1992. 50-60.

---. "Exegesis of Matthew 19:3-9." *The Spiritual Sword: What Do the Scriptures Say About Divorce and Remarriage?* 28:4 (1997): 3-8.

---. "Key Scriptures: Matthew 19:3-12." *Marriage, Divorce, and Remarriage (1992 Spiritual Sword Lectureship).* Ed. Jim Laws. Memphis, TN: Getwell, 1992. 338-363.

Highers, Alan E. "The Importance of This Study." *The Spiritual Sword: What Do the Scriptures Say About Divorce and Remarriage?* 28:4 (1997): 1-2.

Laws, Jim. "Attitudes We Should Possess Toward God, His Word, and One Another." *Marriage, Divorce, and Remarriage (1992 Spiritual Sword Lectureship).* Ed. Jim Laws. Memphis, TN: Getwell, 1992. 11-26.

Lipe, David. "How to Properly Interpret the Bible." *Your Marriage Can Be Great.* Ed. Thomas B. Warren. Jonesboro, AR: National Christian Press, 1978. 79-86.

Rader, Donnie V. *Marriage, Divorce and Remarriage.* Bowling Green, KY: Guardian of Truth Foundation, 2003.

Thomas, J.D. *Divorce and Remarriage.* Abilene, TX: Biblical Research Press, 1977.

Chapter 2: God's OVER-View of Marriage & Divorce

I. **Appreciating MARRIAGE As a Divine Institution**
   A. **Marriage was created by God, as detailed in Genesis 2.**
      1. God created the man (2:7) and the woman (2:21-22), creating them for each other.
      2. God created marriage in the beginning, when "He brought her to the man" (2:22).
      3. Thus, it is God alone, not man, who has the right to govern all things marriage-related.
   B. **Marriage is regulated by God in His Word.**
      1. Scripture gives "us all things that pertain to life and godliness" (2 Pet. 1:3).
      2. Marriage, by God's creation, incorporates both of these elements (life & godliness).
      3. As soon as God created marriage, He gave the principles to govern it (Gen. 2:24).
      4. Jesus used the same words, showing the timeless nature of God's regulation (Mt. 19:5).
      5. The Holy Spirit had Paul to quote the same principles again in Ephesians 5:22-33.
      6. Marriage has existed "from the beginning" (Mark 10:6), and so have God's laws.
   C. **Marriage is defined by God in His Word.**
      1. God's Word defines marriage as (adapted from Flavil Nichols):
         (a) The lifelong
         (b) Covenant (contract or commitment)
         (c) According to the law of God
         (d) And the laws of the land
         (e) Between two eligible persons
         (f) Of opposite sex (one male and one female)
         (g) Who become one with each other
         (h) With the privilege of sexual cohabitation
         (i) And the obligation to agape love one another
         (j) Until separated (disjoined) by death.

II. **Understanding MARRIAGE in God's Eyes (The Only View That Matters!)**
   A. **God Gave the Plan for Marriage: The Only Plan That Matters!**
      1. Most conflict over MDR could be prevented & resolved if learn & accept God's plan.
      2. God's plan today is the same plan He had at the beginning (Mark 10:6-9).
      3. God is the one who established the divine and sacred relationship of marriage.
   B. **God Gave the Participants for Marriage.**
      1. "From the beginning of the creation, God 'made them male and female'" (Mk. 10:6).
         (a) "Male and female He created them" (Gen. 1:27).
         (b) When God made a mate for the man, He created woman. That's God's plan!
      2. Monogamy (one male and one female) is authorized, not polygamy.
         (a) "...the two shall become... (Mt. 19:5). There are only two = one man, one woman.
         (b) 1 Cor. 7:2; 9:5; Eph. 5:23-33 – Spouses are always referred to as singular.
      3. Heterosexuality (a male with a female) is authorized, not homosexuality.
         (a) Gen. 1:27; Matt. 19:4; Lev. 18:22; 20:13; Rom. 1:26-32; 1 Cor. 6:9
         (b) Marriage, in God's eyes, is always between a man and a woman.
            (1) God joins a "man" to "his wife." He does not approve any other "union."
         (c) Every reference to homosexuality in Scripture is always condemned.

4. God, who alone can regulate marriage, restricts those who can enter marriage:
   (a) A person who has never been married (1 Cor. 7:28; 9:5)
   (b) A person who has been married but whose spouse is dead (Ro. 7:2-3; 1 Cor. 7:39).
   (c) A person once married but whose spouse was put away for fornication (Mt. 19:9).
5. Of course, both parties in a marriage must be eligible in God's sight to marry.

C. **God Gave the Priority for Marriage.**
1. The husband-wife bond is to take precedence over all other earthly relationships.
2. This requires decisiveness – "a man shall leave his father and mother" (Gen. 2:24).
   (a) What was once a man's closest relationship must now yield to his marriage.
   (b) Loyalty to one's spouse must take precedence over loyalty to father or mother.
   (c) The man and woman must understand the importance of their decision.
3. This requires commitment – "and shall cleave unto his wife" (Gen. 2:24)
   (a) "Cleave" = "to join fast together, to glue, cement," stick together no matter what!
   (b) This is an exclusive and continuing commitment.
4. This requires unity – "and they shall become one flesh" (Gen. 2:24).
   (a) "One flesh" emphasizes a special kind of union between husband and wife:
      (1) The totalities of two lives are joined together into one life with one goal.
      (2) Become one physically, spiritually, emotionally, socially, psychologically, etc.
      (3) "This is now bone of my bones and flesh of my flesh" (Gen. 2:23).
   (b) For two to become one, each must surrender part of themselves.
      (1) "I"→"We" + "Me"→"Us" + "My"→"Our" + "Mine"→"Ours"
   (c) Marriages begin to weaken when a "two" begins to take priority over the "one."
5. This requires exclusivity – "They were both naked, the man and his wife" (Gen. 2:25).
   (a) Husbands and wives must demonstrate absolute fidelity to each other.
6. This requires a higher loyalty – "out of reverence for Christ" (Eph. 5:21, ESV).
   (a) The marriage relationship must share a mutual allegiance first to Jesus Christ!

D. **God Gave the Provisos for Marriage.**
1. There must be intention to live together as husband and wife (Matt. 19:5-6).
   (a) Leaving parents and cleaving to one's mate denotes an agreement to be married.
2. There must be a commitment to each other (Gen. 2:24).
   (a) There must be a vow of devotion to each other, especially for spiritual purposes.
3. There must be compliance with the laws of the land or the society in which one lives.
   (a) Christians must obey the laws of the land (Rom. 13:1-7).
   (b) Whatever the laws of the land require for marriage, Christians must comply
       (unless they violate the revealed will of God, which must come first—Acts 5:29).
4. There must be love for and submission to one another (Eph. 5:22-25, 28; 1 Pet. 3:1).
   (a) *Agape* love must dominate the marriage & permeate all aspects of it (1 Co. 13:4-7).
   (b) Cohabitation does not equate to marriage (Heb. 13:4; John 4:18; Matt. 1:25).

E. **God Gave Purpose to Marriage.**
1. To provide self-completion and wonderful companionship (Gen. 2:18).
   (a) Not good to be alone; incomplete without the other; need one "comparable."
2. To enjoy sexual intimacy and fulfillment (Gen. 2:25; 1 Cor. 7:1-5; Heb. 13:4).
   (a) Marriage is the only divinely authorized situation for a man and woman to have sex.
   (b) Husbands & wives are "husband and wife" at the end of the marriage ceremony.
   (c) Each spouse has the exclusive right to the body of his/her mate, to be "one flesh."
3. To propagate the human race (Gen. 1:27-28).
   (a) Multiply a godly offspring (Mal. 2:15) and teach them diligently (Deut. 6:7).

4. To prevent or avoid fornication, sexual immorality (1 Cor. 7:2-4)
5. To help each other get to heaven (1 Cor. 7:14, 16; 1 Pet. 3:1, 7).
6. To promote better understanding of Christ's relationship to the church (Eph. 5:22-33).

F. **God Gave Permanence to Marriage.**
1. God's general law of marriage is that it is for life (Mk. 10:9-12; Ro. 7:2-3; 1 Co. 7:10-11).
2. From the beginning, marriage was to be a permanent bond.
    (a) "Leave father and mother" does not ever have returning in view. It's permanent!
    (b) "Cleave unto his wife" does not ever have "un-cleaving" in view. It's permanent!
    (c) "Shall become one flesh" does not ever have "two flesh" in view. It's permanent!
3. Jesus emphatically affirmed the permanency of marriage.
    (a) Jesus contrasted the popular view of His day (end marriage for any reason).
    (b) Jesus taught "leaving," "cleaving" and two becoming "one flesh" (Matt. 19:5).
    (c) Jesus taught, "They are no longer two but one flesh" (Matt. 19:6).
    (d) Jesus taught, "God has joined together" AND "Let not man separate" (Mt. 19:6).
4. God intended (and still intends) for marriage to last until death separates them.
    (a) God planned for marriage to be for life!
    (b) "The woman who has a husband is bound by the law to her husband as long as he lives. But if the husband dies, she is released from the law of her husband" (Ro. 7:2).
    (c) "A wife is bound by law as long as her husband lives" (1 Cor. 7:39).
    (d) Leaving, cleaving and weaving two lives together, in God's eyes, is irrevocable!

III. **Understanding DIVORCE in God's Eyes (The Only View That Matters!)**
A. **The N.T. Greek word for divorce is *apoluo*.**
1. "Set free, release; let go, send away, dismiss" – often of setting someone free.
2. It is often translated, "put away," involving a mental, intentional, then legal act.
B. **Marriage involves a contract/covenant between three parties: man, woman, God.**
1. If marriage involves more than just the two human parties, then divorce also must involve more than just the two human parties.
2. If the only marriages "acceptable" to God are ones He joins together, then, it would seem to follow that, the only divorces "acceptable" to God are ones He disjoins.
3. If three parties are involved in proper marriages, One cannot be omitted during divorce. Only God can "join" and only God can "disjoin."
C. **God's plan for marriage (from the beginning) never included or intended divorce at all.**
1. From the beginning, God's design for marriage was for one man and one woman to become one flesh and remain together for one lifetime.
2. While there was a temporary "concession" ("permitting" and "suffering" divorce for a time) such was not commanded, required or desired by God. Hence, when Jesus came and taught on the matter, He restored God's original plan from the beginning.
3. God's view of divorce is simple, yet strong – "He hates divorce" (Mal. 2:16)!
4. For a spiritual view of God's view of violating marital fidelity, Read Ezekiel 16.
D. **God's marriage laws are not bound, loosed or altered by what man approves or legislates.**
1. God's divine law is not subservient to civil law! Ever!
    (a) We are to "submit...for the Lord's sake to every human institution" (1 Pet. 2:13).
    (b) But, when human law is not in harmony with divine law, God's law trumps (Ac. 5:29).
    (c) Human/Civil law only has authority that God has provided it (Ro. 13:4; Jn. 19:11).
    (d) Human law has no power to *sanction a wrong* or *forbid something that's right*.
    (e) While civil law differs from culture-to-culture and will change even within a single culture, God's law remains constant and consistent.

2. If civil law joins two people together, that does not mean that God has joined them.
   (a) Just because a marriage is "legal" (to man) does not mean it is Scriptural (to God).
   (b) Just because two people marry does not mean they had a right to marry.
   (c) Herod "married" Herodias (legally), but it wasn't lawful in God's eyes (Mk. 6:17-18).
3. If civil law disjoins two people, that does not mean that God has disjoined them.
   (a) Just because a divorce is "legal" (to man) does not mean it is Scriptural (to God).
   (b) Just because a divorced person remarries does not mean they had a right to do it.

E. **God's general rule regarding marriage, divorce and remarriage:**
   1. "Whoever divorces and marries another commits adultery" (Mark 10:11-12).
   2. If "marries another" while the spouse lives, will be called an adulterer/ess (Ro. 7:3).
   3. If one "does depart, let him/her remain unmarried or be reconciled" (1 Cor. 7:11).
   4. If his/her spouse "dies," he/she "is at liberty to be married" (1 Cor. 7:39).
   5. This was God's original plan for marriage – a lifelong commitment (cf. Mal. 2:16)!
   6. Therefore, the divine rule is that a second marriage is not acceptable but is sinful!
   7. If no divine exception, there could be NO divorce and remarriage without adultery.
   8. The ONLY divine exception is a mate who puts away mate for fornication (Mt. 19:9).

F. **God allows only one exception to His general rule for MDR (Matt. 19:9; 5:31-32).**
   1. If divorce was acceptable to God for any/every cause, then His laws are meaningless.
   2. In marriage, neither spouse has a God-given right to break their union to each other.
   3. The ONE exception that God permits to His general rule of "marriage for life, no divorce," is the intrusion of a third party that strikes at the heart this God-ordained "one-flesh union" – i.e., when a spouse takes that "one flesh" outside the marriage.
   4. If one's spouse is guilty of fornication, the innocent spouse has a God-given right to break the union & marry another without committing adultery. Only one exception!

IV. **Understanding FORNICATION in God's Eyes (The Only View That Matters!)**
   A. Fornication is a broad term that includes all other illicit sexual activity.
   B. The Greek *porneia* means, "every kind of unlawful sexual intercourse" (BDAG).
   C. It includes sex between unmarried people (1 Cor. 7:2), between individuals who may be married but not to each other (Matt. 19:9), homosexuality (Jude 7) and bestiality.

V. **Understanding ADULTERY in God's Eyes (The Only View That Matters!)**
   A. Adultery is a specific type of fornication—at least one party is married to someone else.
   B. The Greek *moicheia* means, "unlawful intercourse with the spouse of another."
   C. One can "live in adultery" (continuous sin) when God views the first marriage still binding.

VI. **Understanding REPENTANCE in God's Eyes (The Only View That Matters!)**
   A. Repentance is a "change of mind" that leads to "change of conduct." More than sorrow.
   B. True repentance involves: [1] sorrow for sin (2 Cor. 7:10); [2] change of mind (Matt. 21:29); [3] change of conduct, including discontinuing sinful living (Matt. 3:8; 12:41).

VII. **Accepting God's View and Laws of Marriage**
   A. In a day of disposable marriages and divorce "for every cause":
      1. God's divine rule regarding MDR likely seems harsh to many folks (or most).
      2. To hold to God's restrictive view of marriage can be unpopular and "unloving."
   B. The reaction of Jesus' disciples shows that God's view is intentionally narrow (Mt. 19:10).
   C. Rejection of God's marriage laws, leading one to engage in unscriptural divorces and remarriages, will cost that one (and any new "spouses") a home in heaven.
      1. "Fornicators and adulterers God will judge" (Heb. 13:4).
      2. "Neither fornicators...nor adulterers...will inherit the kingdom of God" (1 Cor. 6:9-10).
   D. Do what God says about marriage (which is straightforward) & you'll have no problems!

BIBLIOGRAPHY
For Chapter 2

(BDAG) Bauer, Walter, F.W. Danker, William F. Arndt, and F. Wilber Gingrich. *A Greek-English Lexicon of the New Testament and Other Early Christian Literature*. 3rd edition. Chicago: University of Chicago Press, 2000.

Deaver, Mac. "The Biblical Definition of 'Fornication' and 'Adultery.'" *Marriage, Divorce, and Remarriage (1992 Spiritual Sword Lectureship)*. Ed. Jim Laws. Memphis, TN: Getwell, 1992. 268-280.

Deaver, Roy. "The Physical Relationship Is <u>Not</u> What Constitutes Marriage." *Your Marriage Can Be Great*. Ed. Thomas B. Warren. Jonesboro, AR: National Christian Press, 1978. 92-93.

Edwards, Earl. "Exegesis of Matthew 19:3-12." *Building Stronger Christian Families (1992 Freed-Hardeman University Lectureship)*. Ed. Winford Claiborne. Henderson, TN: Freed-Hardeman University, 1992. 50-60.

---. "Exegesis of Matthew 19:3-9." *The Spiritual Sword: What Do the Scriptures Say About Divorce and Remarriage?* 28:4 (1997): 3-8.

---. "Key Scriptures: Matthew 19:3-12." *Marriage, Divorce, and Remarriage (1992 Spiritual Sword Lectureship)*. Ed. Jim Laws. Memphis, TN: Getwell, 1992. 338-363.

Elkins, Garland. "Jesus' Teaching on Marriage, Divorce, and Remarriag." *Studies in Matthew*. Ed. Dub McClish. Denton, TX: Valid Publications, 1995. 385-410.

Hazelip, Harold. "Marriage—Its Meaning." *Your Marriage Can Be Great*. Ed. Thomas B. Warren. Jonesboro, AR: National Christian Press, 1978. 94-97.

Highers, Alan E. "What the Scriptures Teach Regarding Marriage, Divorce and Remarriage." *Marriage, Divorce, and Remarriage (1992 Spiritual Sword Lectureship)*. Ed. Jim Laws. Memphis, TN: Getwell, 1992. 27-38.

Hogan, Norman. "God Hates 'Putting Away.'" *Your Marriage Can Be Great*. Ed. Thomas B. Warren. Jonesboro, AR: National Christian Press, 1978. 151-156.

Jackson, Wayne. "Divorce and Civil Law." *Christian Courier*. Web. 11 Nov 2013.

---. "False Ideas About Marriage." *Building Stronger Christian Families (1992 Freed-Hardeman University Lectureship)*. Ed. Winford Claiborne. Henderson, TN: Freed-Hardeman University, 1992. 137-153.

---. *The Teaching of Jesus Christ on Divorce & Remarriage*. Stockton, CA: Courier Publications, 2002.

Jones, Charles. "Key Scriptures: Genesis 2:18-25." *Marriage, Divorce, and Remarriage (1992 Spiritual Sword Lectureship)*. Ed. Jim Laws. Memphis, TN: Getwell, 1992. 297-309.

Jones, Edwin S. "The Biblical Definition of Divorce." *Marriage, Divorce, and Remarriage (1992 Spiritual Sword Lectureship)*. Ed. Jim Laws. Memphis, TN: Getwell, 1992. 254-267.

Lanier, Roy H. Sr. "What Is Marriage?" *Your Marriage Can Be Great.* Ed. Thomas B. Warren. Jonesboro, AR: National Christian Press, 1978. 89-91.

Lusk, Maurice W., III. "Fornication—Its Meaning." *Your Marriage Can Be Great.* Ed. Thomas B. Warren. Jonesboro, AR: National Christian Press, 1978. 105-109.

Nichols, Flavil H. "The Biblical Definition of Marriage." *Marriage, Divorce, and Remarriage (1992 Spiritual Sword Lectureship).* Ed. Jim Laws. Memphis, TN: Getwell, 1992. 241-253.

Pryor, Neale. "Divorce—Its Meaning." *Your Marriage Can Be Great.* Ed. Thomas B. Warren. Jonesboro, AR: National Christian Press, 1978. 98-104.

Rader, Donnie V. *Marriage, Divorce and Remarriage.* Bowling Green, KY: Guardian of Truth Foundation, 2003.

Shannon, John. "What Our Young People Need to Know About Marriage." *Marriage, Divorce, and Remarriage (1992 Spiritual Sword Lectureship).* Ed. Jim Laws. Memphis, TN: Getwell, 1992. 166-185.

Taylor, Robert R., Jr. "Crucial Questions Asked About Marriage." *Marriage, Divorce, and Remarriage (1992 Spiritual Sword Lectureship).* Ed. Jim Laws. Memphis, TN: Getwell, 1992. 54-73.

Thomas, J.D. *Divorce and Remarriage.* Abilene, TX: Biblical Research Press, 1977.

Vine, W.E. *Vine's Complete Expository Dictionary of Old and New Testament Words.* Nashville: Nelson, 1996.

Warren, Thomas B. "A General Look at Divorce & Remarriage." *The Spiritual Sword: Marriage, Divorce, Remarriage.* 6:2 (1975): 1-9.

---. "Only Three Classes of People Are Free (In the Sight of God) to Marry." *Your Marriage Can Be Great.* Ed. Thomas B. Warren. Jonesboro, AR: National Christian Press, 1978. 353-355.

Woodson, William. "Whoever Shall Marry Her When She Is Put Away Committeth Adultery." *Your Marriage Can Be Great.* Ed. Thomas B. Warren. Jonesboro, AR: National Christian Press, 1978. 403-409.

Chapter 3: Matthew 19 and God's Original Plan

I. The Setting of Jesus' Teaching in Matthew 19 Is Important to Observe (19:1-2).

    A. Contextually, Jesus had just been teaching about forgiveness (chap. 18) in Galilee (19:1).

    B. Upon departing from Galilee in 19:1, He would not return there again before His death.

    C. He went "to the region of Judea beyond the Jordan" (19:1).

        1. This region of Judea, on the east side of (i.e., "beyond") the Jordan, was called Perea.

        2. Herod Antipas ruled over this region of Judea.

        3. Herod Antipas had beheaded John the Immerser for his teaching on MDR.

            (a) Herod had married his brother's wife, Herodias (Mark 6:17).

            (b) John came preaching over and over, "It is not lawful for you to have her" (6:18).

            (c) While Herod's marriage did not violate civil law, it did violate God's law!

    D. It is not certain, but perhaps that is why the Pharisees chose to ask Jesus about MDR then.

        1. Perhaps they thought they'd get Jesus to say something that would get Him killed, too.

    E. The Pharisees were the largest and most respected sect of the Jewish leaders.

        1. They were revered for their (supposed) knowledge of the law.

        2. Even more so, they were revered for their (supposed) careful adherence to the law.

        3. In reality, the Pharisees had created a system of traditions that superseded the law.

        4. They were more concerned with their traditions and interpretations than with truth.

        5. The motivation of the Pharisees who came to Jesus was to "test Him" (19:3).

            (a) They sought opportunities to impair His credibility with the people.

            (b) They sought opportunities to create trouble for Him, even life-threatening trouble.

II. The Pharisees' Question Gives Insight into the Teaching and Practice of That Day (19:3).

    A. Repeatedly testing Him, "Is it lawful for a man to divorce his wife for just any reason?"

        1. This was not an honest question from the Pharisees seeking an honest answer.

        2. They were not seeking truth; they were seeking to trick and catch Jesus in a fix.

    B. The word "divorce" needs to be understood properly.

        1. The Greek word is *apoluo,* meaning "send away, dismiss, divorce."

        2. ASV & KJV usually translate it, "put away," involving a mental and intentional act.

        3. NKJV, NASB & ESV usually translate it "divorce."

        4. While it involves the civil courts, divorce is more than a civil action.

    C. Their interest in "lawful" had to do with the Law of Moses and not the Law of God.

        1. They wanted to know what Jesus would teach (parallel or contrary) about the law.

        2. Of course, "lawful" in the Pharisees' mind also had more to do with their doctrines.

    D. The real emphasis of the question is at the end, "...for just any reason?"

        1. ASV: "...for every cause?"; NASB: "...for any reason at all?"; ESV: "...for any cause?"

        2. They were not asking if divorce was lawful; they were asking what reasons were lawful.

        3. Divorce was common and accepted among the Jews, even for trifle reasons.

    E. There were two major (and heatedly contested) schools of thought regarding "cause."

        1. Their divide was based upon differing interpretations of Deuteronomy 24:1-4.

            (a) Specifically, the divide was over the meaning of "uncleanness/indecency" (24:1).

            (b) Whatever this was, in their minds, provided acceptable grounds for divorce.

            (c) The Hebrew term, somewhat vague, means, "nakedness of a thing."

            (d) It likely involved some indecent or lewd act, but exactly what it meant is not known.

2. The two major schools of thought followed the positions held by two Rabbis.
   (a) The school of Shammai taught divorce was only lawful for lewdness or worse.
      (1) They emphasized the "nakedness" part of the meaning.
      (2) Some of them may have limited it to adultery, others to a lewd/indecent act.
   (b) The school of Hillel taught that divorce was lawful for every cause.
      (1) They emphasized the more "generic" part of the meaning – "some thing."
      (2) Thus, divorce was allowed (by the Jews) for the smallest of reasons.
      (3) This was the more popular view & more widely "practiced" among the Jews.
3. As we will see below, Deuteronomy 24 was not God's law approving divorce.
   (a) It was God's law restricting divorce and trying to get their practice under control.
   (b) It was intended to provide protection for the Jewish wives.

III. Jesus' Response to the Pharisees Was a Restoration of the Original Plan of God (19:4-6).
   A. The Pharisees wanted to see if Jesus would side with Shammai or Hillel.
      1. They wanted to see with whose interpretation of Deuteronomy 24 Jesus would align.
      2. Little did they realize that they were about to be schooled!
      3. The Lord of all man was not obligated to side with any manmade doctrine! Only His!
   B. Jesus charged the Pharisees for their ignorance of God's original intent for marriage.
      1. To Pharisees who took pride in their "knowledge," Jesus said, "Have you not read?"
   C. While the Pharisees argued over Deuteronomy 24, Jesus went back beyond it (19:4-5).
      1. He went back before Moses, before their traditions and before their rabbis.
      2. Jesus went all the way back to God's design for marriage "at the very beginning."
         (a) He could do that, for He was God…He was there…and He knew God's design!
         (b) Jesus created all things (John 1:3; Col. 1:16), including man and woman.
         (c) Therefore, Jesus created marriage and knew the Creator's original design.
         (d) Jesus taught there was marriage "from the beginning of the creation" (Mk. 10:6).
      3. Jesus quoted Genesis 1:27 & 2:24 to answer, "Is it lawful to divorce for any reason?"
         (a) Divorce was not part of God's original plan, for He only created one man for one woman (or one woman for one man). There were no other possible mates!
         (b) Divorce was not part of God's original plan, for they were to "cleave" to each other, with "glue, cement" that made a permanent union.
   D. Jesus emphasized the "one flesh" nature of marriage (19:6).
      1. Jesus used the word "So" to draw a conclusion regarding the bond that had resulted.
      2. "So then, they are no longer two but one flesh."
         (a) In marriage, God takes two persons & makes one. One person cannot be divided.
         (b) Divorce was not part of God's original plan, for it violates the will of God, as it severs the unity that He created in marriage.
   E. Jesus summarized & underscored the respect that man must have for God's marriage (19:6).
      1. In a Scriptural marriage, God joins together (or yokes together) husband and wife.
      2. Who is man to undo what God has done? To disjoin what God has joined?
      3. Proper respect for marriage: "What God has joined together, let not man separate."
         (a) "Let not man separate" is a present tense imperative verb (preceded by "not").
         (b) The actual command (in Greek) is for man to "*stop* doing what he is doing."
            (1) Even the "most religious" of that day were disregarding God's original plan.
            (2) Jesus commanded them to "stop it!" *Stop disjoining what God joins!*
            (3) Regardless of civil law, religious tradition or human desires, follow God's will!

IV. The Pharisees Mistakenly Thought They Had Jesus Cornered & in Conflict with Moses (19:7-8).

    A. In verse 7, they asked (not seeking truth or understanding, but continuing to test Him):

        1. "Why then did Moses command to give a certificate of divorce, and to put her away?"

            (a) They presumed Jesus was wrong, because what He said contradicted Moses.

            (b) However, they had perverted Moses to wrongly justify any cause for divorce.

        2. The Jews had erroneously concluded that Moses "commanded" divorce.

            (a) They had taken Deuteronomy 24:1-4 as God-given right to & support of divorce.

            (b) Such perversion of Deuteronomy 24 had led to rampant divorce among Jews.

        3. Deuteronomy 24:1-4 was simply addressing possible conditions that could occur and what to do when/if they did occur. God was not saying, "It's ok. Go and do it."

            (a) This is a clear case of "casuistic law," which uses "if...then" clauses.

                (1) Casuistic law is not commands or showing approval for things that happen.

                (2) Casuistic law is what must be done when certain things (the "ifs") happen.

                (3) Technically, the "if" clause is the protasis; the "then" (main) clause is the apodosis.

                (4) In Deuteronomy 24, verses 1-3 contain the protases & verse 4 is the apodosis.

            (b) Examples of casuistic law in everyday life:

                (1) Sign in store: "If you break it, you buy it." (not command/permission to break)

                (2) Parent to child: "If you get in a wreck, call the police." (not command to wreck)

            (c) Examples of casuistic law others Scriptures:

                (1) "If he takes another wife, he shall not diminish her food..." (Ex. 21:10).

                (2) "If you buy a Hebrew servant, he shall serve six years..." (Ex. 21:2).

                (3) "If a man steals an ox...and slaughters it or sells it, he shall restore" (Ex. 22:1)

                (4) "When a man goes to the woods...and the head slips from the handle and strikes his neighbor so that he dies, he shall flee to one of these cities" (Dt. 19:5).

            (d) Deuteronomy 24:1-3 are the conditions (not approved) that could occur (the "ifs").

                (1) A man gives wife certificate of divorce for "uncleanness" and sends her away.

                (2) The woman goes and becomes another man's wife.

                (3) The second husband also divorces the woman or he dies.

            (e) Deuteronomy 24:4 is what must be done if the (unacceptable) conditions occur.

                (1) The first husband "is not allowed to take her again to be his wife."

                (2) God did not approve of the first divorce or of the second marriage, for it says:

                    (i) "she has been defiled" (see also Jer. 3:1; Lev. 18:20; Num. 5:13).

                    (ii) "that is an abomination before the Lord" (cf. Lev. 18:24-30; 19:29; Nu. 35:33-34)

            (f) In Deuteronomy 24, God wanted the rampant practice of divorce under control.

                (1) He wanted to dissuade the Jews from divorcing for any and every cause.

                (2) He wanted to make men think hard about divorce, as no reconciliation allowed.

                (3) He wanted to protect the wife, who was often "handled" harshly & severely.

                (4) He was not encouraging, commanding or approving divorce. How could He?

                (5) Compare also Leviticus 21:7, 14; 22:13; Numbers 30:9.

        4. The "uncleanness/indecency" in Deuteronomy 24:1 is somewhat difficult to define.

            (a) Hillel wanted it to include "any cause at all," but it seems more substantial than that.

            (b) Shammai may have wanted it to be adultery, but it was "less" than that.

            (c) It couldn't have been sexual infidelity, for that led to death penalty (Dt. 22:22).

            (d) It was likely some immoral indecency or character flaw, short of intercourse.

B. In verse 8, Jesus corrected their obvious (and even willful) distortion of Moses' words.
  1. First of all, Moses did not "command" divorce, as they suggested and taught. Rather, Moses "permitted you to divorce your wives."
    (a) The Law only "permitted" (NKJV), "allowed" (ESV), "suffered" (ASV) this action.
    (b) The Law did not command it, and God, for sure, did not want it.
    (c) "Suffered/Permitted" does not denote approval but rather toleration for a time.
  2. God permitted this "because of the hardness of your hearts." Divorce was not His will!
    (a) This was not a part of God's original plan; He allowed a temporary relaxation.
    (b) The reason: their hearts were hardened and rebellious toward God's law.
    (c) For a time, God tolerated other practices (ex: polygamy) which He didn't approve.
    (d) God did not (& could not) close the O.T. without reminder of His will (cf. Mal. 2:16).
  3. Once again, Jesus returned to the original plan: "but from the beginning it was not so."
    (a) Jesus wanted these Jews to know that God's "concession" was only temporary.
    (b) He wanted them to know that God's original intention for marriage did not change.
    (c) Jesus was about to tell them that the temporary accommodation was over.
    (d) "But" contrasts what had been taught & permitted with what He was about to say.
      (1) Notice that verse 9 begins, "And I say to you..."
    (e) "From the beginning" takes it all the way back beyond Moses (cf. Mark 10:6).
    (f) "It was not so" is a perfect tense verb, which is very significant.
      (1) Greek perfect tense indicates a past action with abiding results in the present.
      (2) The emphasis is this: "it was not so" in the past and "it is still not so" today.
      (3) God's will and God's law about marriage is permanent and never went away.
  4. Therefore, the Lord was restoring the marriage relationship back to His original intent.
    (a) As Jesus leads into Matthew 19:9, He was reestablishing God's marriage laws.
    (b) Regardless of what Moses taught or permitted, God's law on MDR is God's law!
    (c) To divorce and remarry for any/every cause results in adultery.
    (d) God allows an innocent spouse to divorce a fornicating spouse, and that's it.

V. It Is Tragically Argued That This Is a "Covenant Passage" and Applies Only to Christians.
  A. This false doctrine will be examined more closely in future chapters.
    1. It is argued (even by some members of the church of Christ) that Jesus' teachings in Matthew 19:9 only apply to husbands and wives who are members of the church.
    2. In an effort to justify and accept adulterous relationships among non-Christians (and to not condemn them or teach that they must sever unscriptural relationships), some are advocating that Matthew 19:9 only applies to those already in the church and already in a "covenant" relationship with God (i.e., a "covenant passage").
  B. Many Scriptural responses can and will be given in future chapters, but let these suffice, for they are based on the context of Matthew 19 before even reaching verse 9.
    1. It is obvious that Jesus was returning to God's original marriage laws, not based upon culture or tradition or concession, but upon eternal divine principles.
    2. As Wayne Jackson says, "There was no church of Christ in the Garden of Eden!"
    3. Wayne Jackson offers this logical argumentation:
      (a) Christ's teaching on marriage was a restoration of Heaven's original plan.
      (b) But God's original plan encompassed mankind as a whole.
      (c) Thus, Christ's teaching on marriage encompasses mankind as a whole.

BIBLIOGRAPHY
For Chapter 3

Edwards, Earl. "Exegesis of Matthew 19:3-12." *Building Stronger Christian Families (1992 Freed-Hardeman University Lectureship).* Ed. Winford Claiborne. Henderson, TN: Freed-Hardeman University, 1992. 50-60.

---. "Exegesis of Matthew 19:3-9." *The Spiritual Sword: What Do the Scriptures Say About Divorce and Remarriage?* 28:4 (1997): 3-8.

---. "Key Scriptures: Matthew 19:3-12." *Marriage, Divorce, and Remarriage (1992 Spiritual Sword Lectureship).* Ed. Jim Laws. Memphis, TN: Getwell, 1992. 338-363.

Jackson, Wayne. *The Teaching of Jesus Christ on Divorce & Remarriage.* Stockton, CA: Courier Publications, 2002.

Jones, Edwin S. "The Biblical Definition of Divorce." *Marriage, Divorce, and Remarriage (1992 Spiritual Sword Lectureship).* Ed. Jim Laws. Memphis, TN: Getwell, 1992. 254-267.

Kizer, Andy. "Key Scriptures: Matthew 5:31-32." *Marriage, Divorce, and Remarriage (1992 Spiritual Sword Lectureship).* Ed. Jim Laws. Memphis, TN: Getwell, 1992. 319-337.

Lewis, Jack P. "From the Beginning It Was Not So." *Your Marriage Can Be Great.* Ed. Thomas B. Warren. Jonesboro, AR: National Christian Press, 1978. 410-419.

McClish, Dub. "Is Matthew 19:9 A Part of the Law of Christ?" *The Spiritual Sword: What Do the Scriptures Say About Divorce and Remarriage?* 28:4 (1997): 32-37.

Powell, Ivie. "Key Scriptures: Deuteronomy 24:1-4." *Marriage, Divorce, and Remarriage (1992 Spiritual Sword Lectureship).* Ed. Jim Laws. Memphis, TN: Getwell, 1992. 310-318.

Pryor, Neale. "Divorce—Its Meaning." *Your Marriage Can Be Great.* Ed. Thomas B. Warren. Jonesboro, AR: National Christian Press, 1978. 98-104.

Rader, Donnie V. *Marriage, Divorce and Remarriage.* Bowling Green, KY: Guardian of Truth Foundation, 2003.

Woodson, William. "Analysis of Matthew 5:31-32." *The Spiritual Sword: What Do the Scriptures Say About Divorce and Remarriage?* 28:4 (1997): 8-12.

---. "Whoever Shall Marry Her When She Is Put Away Committeth Adultery." *Your Marriage Can Be Great.* Ed. Thomas B. Warren. Jonesboro, AR: National Christian Press, 1978. 403-409.

Chapter 4: <u>The Authority & Amenability of Matthew 19:9</u>

I.   The Approach to Matthew 19:9

    A.   The central passage in the N.T. on the subject of divorce & remarriage is Matthew 19:9.

    B.   Jesus was returning man's minds & practices (regarding marriage) to God's original plan.

        1.   God never intended for divorce to be permitted without sin attached.

        2.   God's law about marriage is permanent, never went away & must be followed by all.

II.   The Authority of Matthew 19:9

    A.   The Pharisees did not see Jesus as an authority—they "came to Him, testing Him" (19:3).

        1.   To the Jews, Moses was looked to as their authority (19:7).

    B.   Jesus took His opponents back to "the beginning" twice to emphasize original authority (4, 8).

        1.   The context of Matthew 19:1-12 is rich in contrasts:

            (a) Contrast between Jesus and the Pharisees.

            (b) Contrast between the school of Hillel and the school of Shammai.

            (c) Contrast between divorce for any cause and divorce for only one cause.

            (d) Contrast between the law of man (civil) and the law of God (divine/superior).

            (e) Contrast between "put away" and "certificate of divorce."

            (f) Contrast between God's will "at the beginning" & man's willfulness "at present."

            (g) Contrast between two becoming one and one becoming two (again).

            (h) Contrast between God joining together and man putting asunder.

            (i) Contrast between Moses commanding and Moses permitting.

            (j) Contrast between hardness of hearts and making oneself a eunuch for Christ.

            (k) Contrast between what the Pharisees/Rabbis/Moses said and what "I say to you."

    C.   The authority in Matthew 19:9 is Jesus Himself!

        1.   After they tested Jesus and twisted the Scripture, Jesus finally said, "I say to you."

            (a) This is the first use of the first person singular pronoun in this context.

        2.   Notice that His authority is divine and reaches back to the beginning.

            (a) "**He who** made them at the beginning" (19:4; cf. Col. 1:16).

            (b) "What **God** has joined together" (19:6; cf. John 1:3).

            (c) "From **the beginning**" (19:8; cf. John 1:1).

        3.   Jesus contrasted man's authority and Moses' authority with His/Divine authority!

            (a) "**And I say to you**" (19:9; cf. 5:32).

            (b) Moses <u>was</u> the lawgiver (cf. Jn. 1:17); <u>now</u> Christ is the lawgiver (1 Co. 9:21; Ga. 6:2).

    D.   Matthew 19:9 is God's law on marriage, divorce and remarriage.

III.   The Amenability of Matthew 19:9

    A.   To alter amenability to Matthew 19:9, some try altering the amenability of Matthew 19:9.

        1.   The clarity of Jesus' teaching in Matthew 19:9 could not be clearer.

            (a) This is not a difficult verse to understand. Its terms & grammar are not complex.

            (b) When Scripture disagrees with one's life, some wish to alter Scripture instead of life.

            (c) With the increase in divorce comes an increase in those seeking to justify remarriage.

        2.   The force (and restrictiveness) of Jesus' teaching in Matthew 19:9 is obvious.

            (a) Anyone who divorces and remarries commits adultery (only one exception).

            (b) Anyone who has been put away & then remarries commits adultery (no exceptions).

            (c) Anyone who marries someone who is put away commits adultery (no exceptions).

(d) Only the innocent party (whose spouse was unfaithful) may divorce and remarry.

(e) True repentance necessitates severing all sinful relationships.

(f) The clarity & severity of Jesus' words was recognized by the apostles present (19:10).

(g) The clarity of truth is too clear and the force too obvious for some to accept.

3. To dismiss the forcefulness & restrictiveness of Matt. 19:9, some have crafted falsehoods.

    (a) From one extreme: Matt. 19:9 is not part of N.T. law & doesn't apply to Christians.

    (b) To another extreme: Matt. 19:9 is a covenant passage that only applies to Christians.

    (c) Try to escape inescapable truth and justify adulterous marriages than accept truth.

    (d) Let's examine and answer each of these carefully.

B. False amenability doctrine: **Matthew 19:9 is not amenable to Christians.**

1. Advocates argue that the N.T. took effect on Pentecost in Acts 2, and therefore, anything stated in the Bible before Acts 2 (incl. Mathew 19:9) is not part of the N.T.

    (a) They claim Matthew, Mark, Luke, John & Acts 1 are not part of the new covenant.

        (1) As the "last O.T. prophet," Jesus lived under the old law (not the New), and what He taught was part of the old law (and not the New), for He had to keep the Old perfectly and could not alter it with any "new" teaching.

        (2) Jesus' teachings were merely explanatory of the Law of Moses.

        (3) Therefore, since the law was nailed to the cross, Jesus' teachings were as well.

    (b) They claim the law for the church (Christians) was not given until Pentecost & after.

        (1) If anything Jesus taught was part of the N.T., it must be stated again after Acts 2.

        (2) Therefore, they will not accept as law anything in the Bible before Acts 2.

    (c) Their motivation is the removal of the "exception clause" from N.T. doctrine.

        (1) In their minds, the exception in Matthew 19:9 is not repeated after Acts 2.

        (2) Therefore, they argue that the exception clause is not law for us today.

    (d) This doctrine (Matthew 19:9 is not amenable to Christians) is blatantly false!

2. Answering this false doctrine with the truth is necessary and fairly simple.

    (a) Truth: To reject one verse/doctrine (i.e., Matthew 19:9) as part of the N.T.:

        (1) Necessarily requires the rejection of the entire chapter (19) & book (Matthew).

        (2) Necessarily requires the rejection of all four gospel accounts as part of N.T.

    (b) Truth: Jesus came to both fulfill the Old and to establish the New. He did both!

        (1) "I did not come to destroy [the Law or the Prophets] but to fulfill" (Mt. 5:17).

        (2) "...the word that I have spoken will judge him in the last day" (John 12:48).

    (c) Truth: While Jesus did explain parts of the Law of Moses, He also taught the New.

        (1) Are verses like these part of the Old (i.e., Jesus explaining it) or part of the New?

            (i) John 3:3, 5 – "unless one is born again, he cannot see the kingdom of God"

            (ii) Matthew 19:28 – apostles "will sit on twelve thrones, judging Israel"

            (iii) John 14:6 – "No one comes to the Father but by Jesus."

            (iv) Matthew 28:18-20 – "Make disciples of all the nations."

            (v) Mark 16:15-16 – "Preach the gospel to every creature."

        (2) Jesus taught many things that were not part of the Law of Moses.

            (i) Many of Jesus' teachings were not found in the Old or bound by the Old.

            (ii) He could not be merely explaining old laws if they were not laws of the Old.

            (iii) To keep the Old perfectly, even Jesus couldn't "add" to it (Dt. 12:32; Pr. 30:6).

            (iv) Therefore, if Jesus' words were bound on anyone, it is on us (after Acts 2).

        (3) Jesus taught many things (binding on us today) not repeated after Acts 2.

            (i) "...to lust for her has already committed adultery in his heart" (Matt. 5:28).

            (ii) "Do not call anyone on earth your father; for One is your Father" (Mt. 23:9).

(iii) Neither of these verses (and many like them) are never repeated after Acts 2.

(iv) Therefore, Jesus' teachings before Acts 2 are part of N.T. & amenable to us.

(d) Truth: Jesus often contrasted the teaching of the Old with His teaching.

  (1) He could not be merely clarifying/explaining the Old if He was differentiating.

    (i) This is seen repeatedly in Matt. 5 (vv. 21-22, 28, 31-32, 33-34, 38-39, 43-44).

    (ii) This is seen even in Matthew 19: "Moses permitted...And I say to you..."

    (iii) While Jesus did provide explanation and interpretation of the Law of Moses on occasion, He also contrasted definitively His law from the Old.

  (2) If Matthew 19:9 merely explained the Law of Moses, then Jesus contradicted it.

    (i) The Law of Moses permitted divorce for "uncleanness" (Deut. 24:1-4).

    (ii) "Uncleanness" could not be adultery, for that meant death (Lev. 20:10).

    (iii) Jesus could not have been explaining the Old, else He was contradicting it.

    (iv) Therefore, Jesus' teachings were different from the Old and thus New.

  (3) Even Pharisees recognized Jesus was contrasting His teaching with Moses (19:7).

(e) Truth: Law can be spoken and taught before it takes effect as law.

  (1) Illustration: Legislatures do this all the time—making laws and explaining laws before those laws take effect.

  (2) Before Acts 2, Jesus taught things that (by His authority) would go into effect later:

    (i) The Great Commission: preach the gospel to save the world (Mark 16:15).

    (ii) The plan of salvation: "He who believes & is baptized will be saved" (16:16).

    (iii) The Lord's Supper: "this is my body...this is my blood" (Matt. 26:26-29).

    (iv) "The kingdom of God" (Luke 16:16): two verses before MDR (Luke 16:18).

    (v) Parables about the kingdom: later established in Acts 2.

    (vi) The work of the apostles and growth of the church in Acts 1:8.

    (vii) Church discipline: *ekklesia* only found twice in gospels (Mt. 16:18; 18:17).

  (3) Before Acts 2, Jesus taught "new" things not authorized in the Law of Moses:

    (i) "All meats clean": something not authorized for the Jews (Mark 7:19).

    (ii) Worship not limited to the mountain, Jerusalem, etc. (John 4:21).

    (iii) Bringing Gentiles into covenant without becoming Jews (Jn. 10:16; 11:47-53).

  (4) Before Acts 2, Jesus taught for men to keep His commandments (Jn. 14:15; 15:14).

    (i) His new law, under His authority, would require a change in the law.

    (ii) Once the old law was removed, His new law took effect.

    (iii) This transition took place at the cross (cf. Col. 2:14; Heb. 7:12; 9:15-17).

  (5) How can Matthew 28, Mark 16, Luke 24, John 21 & Acts 1 not be law today?

    (i) Those who advocate this false position have a hard time being consistent.

    (ii) They don't want Matthew 19:9 to be amenable to them; therefore, they must also eliminate everything else in the N.T. before Acts 2.

(f) Truth: Matthew, Mark, Luke & John were ALL WRITTEN AFTER Pentecost.

  (1) If Jesus' teachings (in Mt, Mk, Lk, Jn) do not apply to us, then to whom?

  (2) If Matthew 19:9 is not amenable to us today, it was never amenable to anyone.

    (i) It was not amenable to the Jews, for fornicators were put to death (Dt. 22:22).

    (ii) It will not be amenable in heaven, for there will be no marriage (Mt. 22:30).

    (iii) Therefore, it is either amenable to us today or it is a meaningless text.

  (3) These books were written by the authority of Christ!

    (i) Would the authority of Christ add to the Law of Moses after it was dead?

    (ii) Or write a book to the Greeks (i.e., Luke) that had nothing to do with them?

C. False amenability doctrine: **Matthew 19:9 is amenable ONLY to Christians.**
  1. Advocates argue that this is a "covenant passage" that is amenable only to husbands and wives who are both Christians (i.e., members of the church).
     (a) Not apply to two non-Christians married or to a Christian married to a non-Christian.
     (b) And, since these individuals are not amenable to it, they cannot commit adultery.
  2. Answering this false doctrine with the truth is necessary and fairly simple.
     (a) Truth: It is obvious that Jesus was returning to God's original marriage laws, not based upon culture or tradition or concession, but upon eternal divine principles.
         (1) These marriage laws embraced the whole of humanity (no church in Eden!).
         (2) Therefore, they are not limited to "covenant people" but extend to all people.
     (b) Truth: There was not a single Christian present when Jesus was speaking.
         (1) There were great multitudes (19:2-3), Pharisees (19:3) & His disciples (19:10).
         (2) If this verse is only amenable to Christians, why was Jesus wasting His breath?
         (3) If His words were not addressed to His Jewish inquirers, He dodged the question.
     (c) Truth: Since those outside the church can commit the sins of fornication and adultery, then the marriage laws of God must apply to them.
         (1) The Christians in Corinth were reminded of their lifestyle before Christ.
             (i) "Neither fornicators...nor adulterers...will inherit the kingdom of God."
             (ii) "And such were some of you" (1 Cor. 6:9-11), before becoming Christians.
             (iii) God says that they were adulterers, but based upon whose law (if they were not subject to the law of God on marriage, divorce & remarriage)?
             (iv) By definition, to be called "adulterers," these non-Christians must have been amenable to God's marriage law before they became Christians!
         (2) God created marriage as His authorized "bed" for sex (Heb. 13:4; 1 Cor. 7:2).
             (i) If non-Christians are not amenable to God's marriage laws, then are they permitted to fulfill their sexual desires in any way or place they want?
             (ii) What verse would teach otherwise?
     (d) Truth: Jesus universally applied His teaching with unlimited application to "whoever."
         (1) "Whoever" is not a word limited by Jesus to Christians in a "covenant."
             (i) "Whoever murders will be in danger of the judgment" (Matt. 5:21).
             (ii) "Whoever is angry with his brother without a cause..." (Matt. 5:22).
             (iii) "Whoever looks at a woman to lust for her..." (Matt. 5:28).
             (iv) "Whoever desires to save his life will lose it..." (Matt. 16:25).
             (v) "Whoever divorces his wife for any reason except..." (Matt. 5:32).
             (vi) Do Jesus' warnings about murder, anger and lust apply to both Christians and non-Christians? Obviously, they do, as do His words in 5:32 & 19:9.
         (2) "Whoever" is used interchangeably by Jesus with "everyone."
             (i) "*Everyone* who is angry with his brother...*whoever* says to his brother" (5:22).
             (ii) "*Whoever* sends his wife away...*everyone* who divorces his wife" (5:31-32).
         (3) Jesus' universal use of "whoever" matches the rest of the N.T.
             (i) "Whoever calls on the name of the Lord shall be saved" (Rom. 10:13).
             (ii) "Whoever desires, let him take the water of life freely" (Rev. 22:17).
     (e) Consider again this logical argumentation from Wayne Jackson:
         (1) Christ's teaching on marriage was a restoration of Heaven's original plan.
         (2) But God's original plan encompassed mankind as a whole.
         (3) Thus, Christ's teaching on marriage encompasses mankind as a whole.
D. **Matthew 19:9 is amenable to all men and all women in all marriages today.**

BIBLIOGRAPHY
For Chapter 4

Deaver, Roy. "Is the Non-Christian Amenable to Christ's Law of Marriage, Divorce, and Remarriage?" *Marriage, Divorce, and Remarriage (1992 Spiritual Sword Lectureship).* Ed. Jim Laws. Memphis, TN: Getwell, 1992. 487-507.

---. "Matthew 19:9 and 1 Corinthians 7." *The Spiritual Sword: Another Look at Marriage, Divorce, Remarriage.* 19:1 (1987): 6-12.

---. "Matthew 19:9 Is a Part of the New Testament." *Your Marriage Can Be Great.* Ed. Thomas B. Warren. Jonesboro, AR: National Christian Press, 1978. 76-78.

---. "Some Errors on 1 Corinthians 7 Set Forth and Refuted." *Your Marriage Can Be Great.* Ed. Thomas B. Warren. Jonesboro, AR: National Christian Press, 1978. 437-453.

Edwards, Earl. "Exegesis of Matthew 19:3-12." *Building Stronger Christian Families (1992 Freed-Hardeman University Lectureship).* Ed. Winford Claiborne. Henderson, TN: Freed-Hardeman University, 1992. 50-60.

---. "Exegesis of Matthew 19:3-9." *The Spiritual Sword: What Do the Scriptures Say About Divorce and Remarriage?* 28:4 (1997): 3-8.

---. "Key Scriptures: Matthew 19:3-12." *Marriage, Divorce, and Remarriage (1992 Spiritual Sword Lectureship).* Ed. Jim Laws. Memphis, TN: Getwell, 1992. 338-363.

Elkins, Garland. "Jesus' Teaching on Marriage, Divorce, and Remarriag." *Studies in Matthew.* Ed. Dub McClish. Denton, TX: Valid Publications, 1995. 385-410.

Jackson, Wayne. *Divorce & Remarriage (A Study Discussion).* Stockton, CA: Courier Publications, 1983.

---. "False Ideas About Marriage." *Building Stronger Christian Families (1992 Freed-Hardeman University Lectureship).* Ed. Winford Claiborne. Henderson, TN: Freed-Hardeman University, 1992. 137-153.

---. *The Teaching of Jesus Christ on Divorce & Remarriage.* Stockton, CA: Courier Publications, 2002.

McClish, Dub. "Is Matthew 19:9 A Part of the Law of Christ?" *The Spiritual Sword: What Do the Scriptures Say About Divorce and Remarriage?* 28:4 (1997): 32-37.

Moffitt, Jerry. "Are All Men Amenable to Christ's Law?" *The Spiritual Sword: What Do the Scriptures Say About Divorce and Remarriage?* 28:4 (1997): 37-40.

Rader, Donnie V. *Marriage, Divorce and Remarriage.* Bowling Green, KY: Guardian of Truth Foundation, 2003.

Taylor, Robert R., Jr. "Crucial Questions Asked About Marriage." *Marriage, Divorce, and Remarriage (1992 Spiritual Sword Lectureship).* Ed. Jim Laws. Memphis, TN: Getwell, 1992. 54-73.

Chapter 5: Matthew 19:9, Adultery & Jesus' One Exception

I. **Considering the Parallel Passages of Matthew 19:9 and Their Unique Emphases**
   A. God's overall rule on MDR is stated in **Mark 10:11 and verse 12**.
      1. "Whoever divorces his wife and marries another commits adultery against her."
      2. "And if a woman divorces her husband and marries another, she commits adultery."
      3. The law applies equally to the man or woman who divorces his/her mate.
      4. The consequences for violating God's marriage law are equal for all – adultery.
   B. God's overall rule on MDR is stated in **Luke 16:18** and includes the put-away spouse.
      1. "Whoever divorces his wife and marries another commits adultery..."
      2. "...and whoever marries her who is divorced from her husband commits adultery."
      3. Again, the consequences for violating God's marriage law apply equally to all.
         (a) The spouse, who does the putting away & then marries another, commits adultery.
         (b) The spouse, who is put away and then marries another, commits adultery.
         (c) The third party, who marries someone who has been put away, commits adultery.
   C. God's overall rule on MDR is stated in **Matthew 5:32** & stresses the gravity of putting away.
      1. "Whoever divorces his wife for any reason except sexual immorality causes her to commit adultery; and whoever marries a woman who is divorced commits adultery."
      2. By putting away his spouse, a husband puts his wife in a tough position:
         (a) Either remain unmarried for the rest of her life, OR
         (b) Marry another man and thus become an adulterer, along with her new husband.
   D. God's overall rule on MDR is stated in **Matthew 19:9** & answers "divorce for every cause."
      1. "Whoever divorces his wife, except for sexual immorality, and marries another, commits adultery; and whoever marries her who is divorced commits adultery."
      2. The Pharisees had asked about putting away a spouse "for every cause."
      3. Jesus authoritatively answered that there is only one cause for divorce & remarriage.

II. **All of the Parallel Passages, including Matthew 19:9, Discuss "Divorce."**
   A. "Divorce" is severely limited and opposed by the words and commands of Jesus.
   B. Divorce was never included or intended in God's original plan for marriage.
   C. The Greek word *apoluo* means "to set free, release; let go, send away, dismiss."
      1. It was used in "releasing" prisoners (Matt. 27:15-26; John 18:39; Acts 4:21-23).
      2. It was used in "sending away" the multitudes (Matt. 14:15-23; 15:32-39).
      3. It was used in "loosing" infirmities (Luke 13:12).
      4. It was used frequently to mean "divorce" or "put away."
   D. In Matthew 19:9, *apoluo* is an aorist tense (simple past action, sometimes summary).
      1. It is subjunctive mood, which notes the potential/conditional nature of an act.
   E. The act of divorce in the N.T. involved a mental consideration, an intentional decision/action and any legal requirements of the land (doesn't mean it was approved by God).
   F. A reminder of God's view of divorce – "He hates divorce" (Mal. 2:16)!

III. **All of the Parallel Passages, including Matthew 19:9, Discuss "Remarriage."**
   A. "Marriage" or "marries another" is severely limited by the words of Jesus.
   B. There is a monumental difference between "married" acceptably in man's sight and "married" acceptably in God's sight – one is carnal, the other is eternal!
      1. In marriage that is acceptable to God, He joins them together (Matt. 19:6).
      2. But, not all marriages that are legal in man's sight are joined together by God.

C. God used human marital terms accommodatingly even when He had not joined them.
    1. To the Samaritan woman, Jesus said, "You have had five husbands" (John 4:18).
        (a) Obviously, not all five of these men were rightly her husband (in God's eyes).
        (b) But, Jesus used that word accommodatingly to make it easier to understand.
        (c) These may have been "marriages" socially, culturally, publicly and legally.
        (d) But, they were not bound (joined) together by God and His law.
        (e) While a "marriage" in man's eyes, it was "adultery" in God's eyes.
    2. Scripture speaks of "an adulteress" who "married another man" (Rom. 7:2-3).
        (a) Obviously, she had no right to "marry" another man (God did not join them).
        (b) But, God used that word accommodatingly to make it easier to understand.
        (c) This may have been a "marriage" socially, culturally, publicly and legally.
        (d) But, they were not bound (joined) together by God and His law.
        (e) While a "marriage" in man's eyes, it was "adultery" in God's eyes.
    3. Scripture says Herod Antipas was "married" to his brother's "wife" (Mark 6:17-18).
        (a) Obviously, another man's "wife" could not be rightly "married" to Herod.
        (b) But, God used those words accommodatingly to make it easier to understand.
        (c) This may have been a "marriage" socially, culturally, publicly and legally.
        (d) But, they were not bound (joined) together by God and His law.
        (e) That is why John the Immerser kept telling Herod, "It is not lawful for you to have your brother's wife" (Mark 6:18). *It is not lawful in God's eyes!*
        (f) Two present tense verbs emphasize the continuous unlawfulness of it:
            (1) "It is not lawful..." (present tense = "it is and keeps on being unlawful")
            (2) "...to have her" (present tense = "to have and to keep on having her")
            (3) There was nothing Herod could do to keep Herodias as his wife!
            (4) We will see in later notes that some have tried to redefine adultery, which would allow adulterous relationships to continue acceptably.
        (g) While a "marriage" in man's eyes, it was "adultery" in God's eyes.
D. As seen in Chapter 2, God restricts those who can enter marriage to:
    1. A person who has never been married (1 Cor. 7:28; 9:5).
    2. A person who has been married but whose spouse is dead (Rom. 7:2-3; 1 Cor. 7:39).
    3. A person once married but whose spouse was put away for fornication (Matt. 19:9).
    4. Of course, both parties in a marriage must be eligible in God's sight to marry.

IV. All of the Parallel Passages, including Matthew 19:9, Discuss "Adultery."
A. From beginning to end, the Bible speaks of "adultery" very clearly & very disparagingly.
    1. In the Old Testament, "adultery" was a seriously vile and contemptible act.
        (a) "You shall not commit adultery" (Ex. 20:14). It was an act one might "commit."
        (b) "The man who commits adultery with another man's wife, he who commits adultery with his neighbor's wife, the adulterer and the adulteress, shall surely be put to death" (Lev. 20:10). It was an act "committed" with another person.
        (c) "Whoever commits adultery with a woman lacks understanding; He who does so destroys his own soul" (Prov. 6:32). It was an act with serious consequences.
        (d) "Adultery" is often equated with "harlotry/prostitution" (Isa. 57:3; Jer. 5:7; 13:27; Ezek. 6:9; 23:43; Hos. 2:2; 4:13-14). It was a sexual act.
    2. In the New Testament, the Lord is just as clear and just as disapproving.
        (a) However, in an attempt to escape the force of the word, some try redefining it.
        (b) They think that redefining (i.e., softening) the word will ease their responsibility.

B. The definition of "adultery" is unambiguous and has been unchanged.
    1. The Hebrew term *na'aph* = "the violation of the marriage relationship whereby either husband or wife has an illicit sexual relationship with a third party" (Renn 15).
    2. The Greek term *moichos* = "unlawful intercourse with the spouse of another" (Vine 14).
    3. Even today, the English word still carries that meaning: "sex between a married person and someone who is not that person's wife or husband" (Merriam-Webster).
    4. "Adultery" involves a married person having sexual intercourse with a third party.
    5. The word "adultery" is sometimes used in Scripture in a figurative sense.
        (a) In the OT, it referred to Israel's unfaithfulness to her husband, God (Jer. 3; Ezek. 16; 23; Hosea).
        (b) In the NT, it referred to Christians' unfaithfulness to their husband, God (Jas. 4:4).
        (c) While figurative, they still denote sordid relations against God with a third party.
C. Yet, some have tried to make "adultery" mean something less than the sexual act.
    1. It is falsely taught by some (in the church) that adultery is simply "covenant-breaking."
        (a) They teach that adultery is not sex but the act of leaving & divorcing one's mate.
        (b) They view adultery as breaking one's marriage covenant at the time of divorce.
        (c) Adultery does not continue into a second marriage, if one apologizes to God.
        (d) As long as the Christian tells God, "I'm sorry," and promises not to break a covenant again, he can remain in the second marriage with God's blessing.
        (e) All sexual activity after that point is pure and acceptable to God.
        (f) It is obvious, by this theory, that they are trying to justify unscriptural marriages.
    2. A few questions that show the fallacious and irresponsible nature of this position:
        (a) When the word "adultery" is used of the Israelites' unfaithfulness to God:
            (1) Could they have simply said, "I'm sorry," and then continue in idolatry?
            (2) If that forgave their sin, wouldn't God have approved of their idolatry?
        (b) What about a man who Jesus said "looks at a woman to lust for her" (Mt. 5:28)?
            (1) What did it mean, "he has already committed adultery with her in his heart"?
            (2) Was he passionately visualizing breaking a covenant with her?
        (c) What about the woman who was "caught in adultery, in the very act" (Jn. 8:3-4)?
            (1) What did the Pharisees catch her doing?
            (2) Did the Pharisees merely catch her "covenant-breaking"?
            (3) If the woman was sorry and forgiven, why did Jesus tell her to sin no more?
        (d) Why does Hebrews 13:4 tie the "marriage bed" to "adulterers"?
            (1) How does an adulterer ("a covenant breaker") defile the marriage bed?
            (2) Of course, God tells us that defiling the bed has to do with sex (Gen. 49:4; 35:22).
            (3) Even when used figuratively, adultery is committed on a bed (cf. Rev. 2:22).
        (e) How did all of the lexicons (without a single exception) get this definition wrong?
D. The true definition of adultery sheds tremendous light on God's view of marriage.
    1. Jesus teaches that whoever divorces and remarries commits adultery.
        (a) But, from man's view, that first marriage is dissolved and over.
        (b) Why would Jesus use a word (adultery) that means one of the parties is married?
        (c) Jesus did not accidentally use the wrong word or change the word's definition!
        (d) Jesus knew exactly what He was teaching!
    2. Jesus also teaches that whoever marries a divorced person commits adultery (Mt. 5:32).
        (a) "A divorced woman" (5:32), one word in Greek, is a perfect passive participle.
        (b) The perfect tense denotes that results of a past action still exist in the present.
        (c) The force of the perfect tense shows she is still a having-been-put-away woman.
        (d) Therefore, the "third party" enters into an adulterous relationship/marriage.

3. The second marriage is adulterous in God's eyes:
   (a) Because that person is still obligated by law to the first marriage (cf. Rom. 7:2-3).
   (b) Because God still sees that spouse bound to His law of marriage by which He joined.
   (c) Because the "third party" has no right to marry one who is still bound by law.
4. The definition of adultery demands these conclusions.

E. It is critical to understand the force of Jesus using the present tense, "commits adultery."
   1. "Commits adultery" is one word in the Greek New Testament *(moichao).*
   2. "Commits adultery" is in the Greek present tense, which denotes continuous action.
      (a) The adultery is not a "one-time" act (like breaking a covenant) and then it's over.
      (b) One who divorces & marries (both aorist tense) "keeps on committing adultery."
      (c) The second marriage is continuous adultery every time they are intimate.
      (d) Therefore, one can "live in adultery," separated from God (1 Cor. 6:9-11; Col. 3:5-7).
   3. If the adultery was just that act of covenant-breaking that a person committed when he divorced his wife, why would Jesus say he was continually committing adultery?
   4. Knowing that Jesus used the present tense answers all sorts of false arguments.

V. Matthew's Account Is the Only One That Discusses the "Exception for Fornication."

A. God's overall rule on MDR is whoever divorces and remarries commits adultery.
B. If no exception was given, there could be NO divorce and remarriage without adultery.
C. In Matthew 19:9 and 5:32, Jesus gives the only reason one may divorce and remarry.
   1. While many folks divorce and remarry for many causes, they stand guilty before God.
   2. Jesus gave one reason a person could remain innocent through divorce & remarriage.
D. In the phrase "except for fornication":
   1. "Except" means "if and only if." There's one and only one exception! This is it!
      (a) In Matthew 5:32, the word for "except" means "apart from" or "saving for."
      (b) There is not another consideration! Period!
   2. "For" is a "marker of basis for an action" (BDAG 364). This can be the only basis!
      (a) In Matthew 5:32, it is extended to "for the reason/cause/motive of..."
      (b) There is no other reason/cause/motive that will be accepted. This is it!
   3. "Fornication" is the only basis/reason for divorce and must be that basis/reason.
E. Jesus gave "fornication" as the only grounds for an innocent party to divorce & remarry.
   1. "Fornication" (from the Greek *porneia)* is a "generic" term:
      (a) It means "every kind of unlawful sexual intercourse...sexual unfaithfulness" (BDAG).
      (b) It includes all sexual activity that is not between a husband & wife joined by God:
         (1) All outside-of-marriage sex between unmarried persons
         (2) All extra-marital sex of a married person (i.e., adultery is a form of fornication)
         (3) All homosexuality, bestiality, incest, pedophilia, etc.
   2. "Fornication," also translated "sexual immorality," must be taken very seriously!
      (a) In God's overall rule for marriage, only death can sever a marriage (Rom. 7:2-3).
      (b) And, He only gave ONE exception to that rule: fornication.
      (c) He viewed becoming one flesh with a third party as the only cause for divorce.
F. In order for an innocent party to have God's approval to divorce and remarry:
   1. He/She must be an innocent party, not having committed fornication himself/herself.
   2. Fornication must be the actual reason/cause for taking the action of divorce.
   3. Fornication is not a reason/cause that can be applied later after a divorce.
      (a) Sometimes after a divorce for "any other cause," a spouse will commit fornication.
      (b) This is not grounds for the other spouse to retroactively apply that to the divorce.
      (c) Fornication as a result of divorce is not the same as fornication as the cause.

BIBLIOGRAPHY
For Chapter 5

(BDAG) Bauer, Walter, F.W. Danker, William F. Arndt, and F. Wilber Gingrich. *A Greek-English Lexicon of the New Testament and Other Early Christian Literature*. 3rd edition. Chicago: University of Chicago Press, 2000.

Colley, Gary. "Analysis of Romans 7:1-4." *The Spiritual Sword: Marriage, Divorce, Remarriage.* 6:2 (1975): 26-28.

Deaver, Roy. "Analysis of Matthew 19:3-12 and a Review of 'Except for Fornication.'" *The Spiritual Sword: Marriage, Divorce, Remarriage.* 6:2 (1975): 14-26.

---. "The 'Guilty Party' Is Not Free (In God's Sight) to Marry Again." *Your Marriage Can Be Great.* Ed. Thomas B. Warren. Jonesboro, AR: National Christian Press, 1978. 369-383.

Duncan, Bobby. "Key Scriptures: Romans 7:1-4." *Marriage, Divorce, and Remarriage (1992 Spiritual Sword Lectureship).* Ed. Jim Laws. Memphis, TN: Getwell, 1992. 364-374.

Edwards, Earl. "Exegesis of Matthew 19:3-12." *Building Stronger Christian Families (1992 Freed-Hardeman University Lectureship).* Ed. Winford Claiborne. Henderson, TN: Freed-Hardeman University, 1992. 50-60.

---. "Exegesis of Matthew 19:3-9." *The Spiritual Sword: What Do the Scriptures Say About Divorce and Remarriage?* 28:4 (1997): 3-8.

---. "Key Scriptures: Matthew 19:3-12." *Marriage, Divorce, and Remarriage (1992 Spiritual Sword Lectureship).* Ed. Jim Laws. Memphis, TN: Getwell, 1992. 338-363.

Elkins, Garland. "Jesus' Teaching on Marriage, Divorce, and Remarriag." *Studies in Matthew.* Ed. Dub McClish. Denton, TX: Valid Publications, 1995. 385-410.

---. "Let None Deal Treacherously Against the Wife of His Youth." *Your Marriage Can Be Great.* Ed. Thomas B. Warren. Jonesboro, AR: National Christian Press, 1978. 148-150.

Jackson, Wayne. *Divorce & Remarriage (A Study Discussion).* Stockton, CA: Courier Publications, 1983.

---. "False Ideas About Marriage." *Building Stronger Christian Families (1992 Freed-Hardeman University Lectureship).* Ed. Winford Claiborne. Henderson, TN: Freed-Hardeman University, 1992. 137-153.

---. *The Teaching of Jesus Christ on Divorce & Remarriage.* Stockton, CA: Courier Publications, 2002.

---. "What Is Adultery?" *The Spiritual Sword: What Do the Scriptures Say About Divorce and Remarriage?* 28:4 (1997): 21-26.

Jobe, Glenn A. "Is Covenant-Breaking Adultery?" *Marriage, Divorce, and Remarriage (1992 Spiritual Sword Lectureship).* Ed. Jim Laws. Memphis, TN: Getwell, 1992. 520-541.

Kizer, Andy. "Key Scriptures: Matthew 5:31-32." *Marriage, Divorce, and Remarriage (1992 Spiritual Sword Lectureship).* Ed. Jim Laws. Memphis, TN: Getwell, 1992. 319-337.

Rader, Donnie V. *Marriage, Divorce and Remarriage.* Bowling Green, KY: Guardian of Truth Foundation, 2003.

Renn, Stephen D. *Expository Dictionary of Bible Words.* Peabody, MA: Hendrickson, 2005.

Vine, W.E. *Vine's Complete Expository Dictionary of Old and New Testament Words.* Nashville: Nelson, 1996.

Woodson, William. "Whoever Shall Marry Her When She Is Put Away Committeth Adultery." *Your Marriage Can Be Great.* Ed. Thomas B. Warren. Jonesboro, AR: National Christian Press, 1978. 403-409.

Chapter 6: <u>The Put-Away Fornicator May Not Remarry!</u>

I. **Some Believe That a Spouse Who Commits Fornication May Be Put Away & Marry Again.**
   A. Some have concluded that if the bond of marriage is dissolved so that the innocent party can remarry, the marriage bond must also be dissolved for the guilty party to remarry.
      1. They argue that if one party is free to remarry (thus being freed from the marriage bond), then the other party must be free (to the same extent) to remarry.
      2. They argue that one party (the guilty) cannot remain subject to a marriage bond from which the other party (the innocent) has been freed.
      3. They argue that the guilty must be equally as free to remarry as the innocent.
      4. This is a faulty assumption and cannot be sustained by Biblical exegesis!
   B. Some have claimed that "except for fornication" must also apply to the guilty party.
      1. They argue that the exception in the first part of Matthew 19:9 carries over to and is implied in the second part of the verse to mean, "Whoever marries her who is divorced (except it was for fornication) commits adultery."
      2. They argue that the exception applies to both the innocent and the guilty, so that it is not adultery to marry a guilty party or for the guilty party to remarry.
      3. This is a faulty assumption and cannot be sustained by Biblical exegesis!
   C. Some, who hold this position, would say that it is not ideal for the guilty party to remarry but that it is not sinful.
      1. Of course, if it is not sinful and they are freed from their first marriage, why would it not be ideal to marry again? Isn't that just a subjective judgment?

II. **The Put Away-Fornicator May Not Remarry: Biblical Authority Will Not Allow It!**
   A. There is NO Scriptural authority for a put-away fornicator to remarry.
      1. Everything we do must be done by (and with) the authority of Christ (cf. Col. 3:17).
         (a) To act without His authority is to act without Him and to sin (cf. 2 John 9).
      2. The New Testament clearly authorizes three categories of persons to marry:
         (a) A person who has never been married (1 Cor. 7:28; 9:5).
         (b) A person who has been married but whose spouse is dead (Ro. 7:2-3; 1 Cor. 7:39).
         (c) A person once married but whose spouse was put away for fornication (Mt. 19:9).
      3. By what or whose authority can a guilty party be authorized to marry?
         (a) There is no passage in the New Testament that authorizes the put-away fornicator to remarry (or the put-away non-fornicator)!
         (b) To suggest that the put-away fornicator has the same right to remarry, as the innocent party, is to go beyond what Scripture explicitly or implicitly teaches.
   B. There is a tremendous difference between how man views marriage & how God views it.
      1. Marriage, in God's eyes, is much more than a civil union or civil contract.
      2. The man (husband) & woman (wife) are not the only two involved in the marriage.
         (a) Marriage is a three-way relationship with (1) God, (2) husband & (3) wife.
            (1) "The Lord has been witness between you & the wife of your youth" (Mal. 2:14).
         (b) God is the one who joins two individuals in marriage (Matt. 19:6).
      3. Therefore, God is the only one who has the right to determine what dissolves the marriage (and what does not) and who has a right to remarry (and who does not).
      4. God is the One who gives the right to marry; God is the One who can take it away.

C. There is a difference between "the marriage" and "the bond."

1. It is possible for one to be "married" to another person (in human terms) but still be "bound" elsewhere and not permitted to be "remarried" (in God's terms).

   (a) "For the woman who has a husband is **bound by the law to her husband** as long as he lives. But if the husband dies, she is released from **the law of her husband**. So then if, while her husband lives, she marries another man, she will be called an adulteress; but if her husband dies, she is **free from that law**, so that she is no adulteress, though she has married another man" (Rom. 7:2-3).

      (1) A divorced person is "bound" BY and TO the LAW of their spouse.

         (i) "The law of the" spouse (ASV)

         (ii) "The law concerning the" spouse (NASB)

         (iii) "The law of marriage" (ESV)

         (iv) The law to which a person promises to be faithful "until death do us part."

         (v) Each spouse surrenders the right to marry another as long as the other lives.

      (2) A divorced person is bound BY and TO the LAW of God:

         (i) In regard to God's divine plan for marriage.

         (ii) For it is to God that a person promises to live faithfully in his/her marriage.

      (3) A parallel passage in 1 Corinthians 7:39 states:

         (i) "A wife is bound by law as long as her husband lives" (NKJV).

         (ii) "A wife is bound as long as her husband lives" (NASB).

         (iii) "A wife is bound to her husband as long as he lives" (ESV).

         (iv) "A wife is bound for so long time as her husband liveth" (ASV).

      (4) Therefore, if an innocent party chooses to put away a fornicating spouse:

         (i) God releases the innocent party from that law (for did nothing wrong),

         (ii) But He does not release the guilty party from that law (for violated it).

   (b) "For John had said to Herod, '**It is not lawful for you to have** your brother's wife'" (Mark 6:18).

      (1) There was a law that Herod had violated.

      (2) To put it another way, there was **a law still binding** that made their relationship adulterous.

2. Civil law might call it a "marriage" but God calls it adultery.

   (a) God does not "loose" the guilty party from "the law of marriage."

   (b) A guilty party remains obligated/bound to all obligations to which he had yielded.

      (1) God does not grant any freedom/liberty from those obligations/laws to guilty.

3. Since God is the One who does the joining (Matt. 19:6):

   (a) God is the One who can keep one "bound" to His law, and

   (b) God is the One who can "loose" and keep one "loosed" from His law.

4. It is possible, since God is in charge and with God all things are possible:

   (a) For one spouse to be bound to the law of God and the other spouse not, and

   (b) For one spouse to be released from the law of God and the other spouse not.

D. The Bible outright forbids the guilty party to remarry.

1. Jesus plainly taught that when a put-away person remarries, God calls it "adultery" every time.

2. "...whoever marries her who is divorced from her husband commits adultery" (Lk. 16:18).

3. "...whoever marries a woman who is divorced commits adultery" (Matt. 5:32).

4. "...whoever marries her who is divorced commits adultery" (Matt. 19:9).

5. The guilty party, along with every other put-away person, is included in this.

III. The Put Away-Fornicator May Not Remarry: Matthew 19:9 Will Not Allow It!

    A. Based upon word studies in Chapters 4 & 5, Jesus' words in Matthew 19:9 literally read:

        1. "And I am saying to you, that every man who shall send (put) away his wife and shall marry another woman, except it be for the one and only cause (reason) of her sexual unfaithfulness, keeps on committing adultery; and the one who has married a having-been-put-away woman keeps on committing adultery."

    B. There are three persons in this passage who keep on committing adultery:

        1. The person who divorces his wife & marries another (save for the cause of fornication).

        2. The person who has married a woman who has been put away by her husband.

        3. The having-been-put-away woman who is married by another man.

    C. There are two divorced persons (implied) in this passage who do not commit adultery:

        1. The person who divorces his wife & marries another (for the cause of fornication).

        2. The person who has been put away and remains unmarried.

        3. Note: A remarried fornicator does not fit in either of these categories.

    D. Simply stated, all who divorce (not for fornication) and remarry are adulterers!

        1. A guilty party cannot divorce for fornication. Jesus said he/she is an adulterer!

        2. Therefore, a spouse who has sex outside of marriage has forfeited the right to remarry.

    E. The Lord's one exception restricts the guilty party from the right to remarry.

        1. Could Mark & Luke's omission of the exception reflect God's true dislike for divorce?

        2. The word "except" provides the ONLY grounds for divorce and remarriage in God's plan.

            (a) "Except" means "if and only if." There's one and only one exception! This is it!

            (b) In Matthew 5:32, the word for "except" means "apart from" or "saving for."

            (c) There is not another consideration! "Except for fornication" commits adultery.

            (d) No person has a right to divorce and remarry, except the one sinned against.

        3. Likewise, the word "except" provides the ONLY means of entering the kingdom.

            (a) In John 3:5, Jesus said, "**Except** one be born of water and the Spirit, he cannot enter into the kingdom of God!"

            (b) There was not another means of entering the kingdom. This was/is the only one!

            (c) By using the word "except," Jesus restricted entrance to this ONE means.

            (d) NO ONE can enter the kingdom by ANY OTHER means. That's what "except" means!

            (e) "Except" is just as exclusive in Matthew 19:9 as it is in John 3:5.

        4. The ONLY grounds by which one can divorce & remarry is fornication of the spouse.

            (a) If the guilty party can also remarry, then Jesus did not mean "except."

            (b) If the guilty party is also excepted, then all are excepted, leaving no exceptions.

            (c) And, if "except" doesn't mean "except" in Matthew 19:9, then it can't in John 3:5.

        5. If both the innocent and guilty parties have a right to remarry:

            (a) Then "except" is meaningless in the teaching of Jesus.

            (b) Then there would be more than one exception, denying the definition of "except."

            (c) Then, how would anyone ever be guilty of "committing" (present tense, continuous action) adultery? Once a person is involved in adultery, that person would become a "guilty party," who would then be free to remarry at will.

            (d) Then, why was Jesus protecting the rights of the innocent in the first part of 19:9?

            (e) Why did Jesus even discuss this at all? It is nonsensical and superfluous.

    F. Unless Jesus contradicts Himself inside one verse, the guilty party has no right to remarry.

        1. Some people miss (intentionally or unintentionally) the force & simplicity of Mark 16:16.

            (a) They argue "be baptized" is not in the second part of the verse, so it isn't necessary.

            (b) However, Jesus plainly states at the beginning those who shall be saved.

(c) The only persons who shall be saved are those who believe and are baptized.

(d) Jesus would not say something in the second part that would contradict the first.

(e) The same is true with Jesus' teaching in Matthew 19:9.

2. There are two forceful and simple conclusions to be drawn from Matthew 19:9.

(a) The ONLY person who has a right in God's eyes to divorce one spouse and marry another spouse is the person whose spouse is guilty of sexual unfaithfulness.

(b) EVERY person who marries any having-been-put-away person commits adultery.

(c) Based on these simple conclusions, the guilty party has NO right to remarry:

(1) The guilty party is not the person who had divorced his spouse and married another spouse for the reason that his spouse was guilty of fornication.

(2) And, the guilty party IS a having-been-put-away person.

3. To argue that the guilty party does have a right to remarry in God's eyes:

(a) Makes Jesus completely contradict Himself just inside one verse!

(b) Makes Jesus say something in the second part of 19:9 that contradicts the first.

(c) Makes Jesus' teaching on marriage, divorce and remarriage absolutely useless!

(d) Makes it nearly impossible for any marriage to not be labeled "Scriptural"!

G. Aligned with the previous point, the exception cannot apply to the first & second clauses.

1. Practically speaking, the exception cannot be applied to both clauses in the verse.

(a) In the first part, Jesus' exception permits only the offended party to div & rem.

(b) If applied in the second part, then Jesus would permit the offending party to rem.

(c) Obviously, from a practical standpoint, that would make Jesus contradict Himself.

(d) Are we ready for the verse to read: "...whoever marries the home-wrecking fornicator does not commit adultery but is perfectly ok in God's eyes"?

2. Grammatically speaking, the exception cannot be applied to both clauses in the verse.

(a) "Except for fornication" is an adverbial clause that modifies the verbs, "divorces and remarries," in the first part of the verse.

(b) The exception clause is NOT repeated in the second part of the verse, and it cannot be proven to be implied. ("Assumption" is not the same as "implication.")

(1) If it was implied, what word would it modify?

(2) Grammatically, an adverbial modifier cannot just be changed into an adjectival modifier to modify the woman who has been put away.

3. Jesus never gave an exception for the put-away fornicator to remarry.

(a) Every put-away person (fornicator or non-fornicator) must remain unmarried.

(b) To teach otherwise makes Jesus contradict Himself and/or speak utter nonsense.

H. The fact that Jesus omits the definite article in the second part forbids the guilty to remarry.

1. Every word in the Bible is inspired of God, down to the smallest words, like "the."

(a) Since God chose every word to put in, He must have chosen the words to leave out.

2. If Jesus used the definite article in the second clause it would have read:

(a) "...and whoever marries THE/THAT woman who is divorced commits adultery."

(b) The definite article would point back to the woman put away for trivial reasons.

(c) This, potentially, might have helped the guilty-party-may-remarry position, by specifying the put-away non-fornicator and leaving the fornicator unmarked.

(d) But, Jesus, by omitting the article, was not specifying any particular woman.

3. Instead, the identity of the "having-been-put-woman" is indefinite.

(a) Meaning, Jesus taught that marrying any put-away woman results in adultery.

(b) And, there is no exception to that! It includes one put away for fornication!

4. Hugo McCord, a Greek scholar wrote: "If the Greek article…were present to point back to the put-away woman of the first clause, then the exceptive phrase could be inferred in the second clause. But, as written, the second clause asserts that no put-away woman is eligible for remarriage" (p. 438).

IV. The Put Away-Fornicator May Not Remarry: Sound & Biblical Rationale Will Not Allow It!

A. If the guilty party can remarry, then the justice & the holy nature of God are impugned.
   1. Is there a heavier obligation on a put-away non-fornicator than a put-away fornicator?
   2. The guilty-party-can-remarry doctrine is affirming the following:
      (a) The spouse who is put away for anything other than fornication cannot remarry.
      (b) And, the spouse who is put away for committing fornication can remarry.
      (c) How does that align with the justice and holiness of God?
   3. The guilty-party-can-remarry doctrine is also affirming the following:
      (a) If a man divorces his wife because she becomes ugly, fat, boring or a Christian:
         (1) She CANNOT remarry!
      (b) If a woman divorces her husband because he is a drunk, addict, violent or bum:
         (1) She CANNOT remarry!
      (c) HOWEVER, if SHE had only had sex with another man (or a woman or an animal):
         (1) She COULD remarry!
      (d) How does that align with the justice and holiness of God?
         (1) What would that say about the holy nature of God and the marriage bed?
   4. Are we truly to believe that a fornicating person put away by his spouse can remarry?

B. If the guilty party can remarry, then there is a premium and profit placed on sin.
   1. The wife and mother of young children (who is physically, verbally & emotionally abused by her non-Christian husband) has no right to divorce & remarry a nice Christian man.
      (a) If she decides to leave her husband at that point, she must remain unmarried.
      (b) She knows that is not what God wants, and she could not support herself alone.
   2. However, suppose this same woman learned from a preacher friend that she would be free from her husband & eligible to remarry if she just had sex with another man.
      (a) With this information that a guilty party has God's blessing to divorce & remarry, this abused woman takes matters into her own hands to protect her children.
      (b) She has sex with another man, makes sure her husband finds out and now she is able to secure the God-approved freedom that she had been wanting.
   3. While advocates of this doctrine may not endorse this scenario, it is valid nonetheless.
   4. Does the God of the Bible place a premium on sin?
      (a) Are there some loopholes (or even outright permissions) whereby one may find profit or reward through sinning and reap benefits from his own wrong?
      (b) Are those who are guilty of sexual unfaithfulness provided greater advantages in God's sight than those who remain sexually faithful?
      (c) God condemns any philosophy that will "do evil that good may come" (Rom. 3:8).
      (d) Instead, God affirms that "whatever a man sows, that he will also reap" (Gal. 6:7).
   5. How many marriages have been held together by the strict teaching of the Lord on MDR?
      (a) How many couples have worked to solve problems due to God's severe law?
      (b) If the guilty party can remarry, wouldn't that discourage solving problems?
      (c) If the guilty party can remarry, wouldn't that encourage more fornication?
      (d) If the guilty party can remarry, wouldn't that tempt unhappy spouses to sin?
      (e) If there is perceived to be lesser penalty (and maybe no penalty at all) for a greater sin and a greater penalty for a lesser sin, wouldn't that support more fornication?

C. If the guilty party can remarry, then it empowers the fornicator to an illogical absurdity.
   1. In Matthew 19:9, "whoever...marries another" is the one who can initiate the divorce.
      (a) Jesus used the coordinating conjunction "and" to join "divorces" and "marries."
      (b) Therefore, whoever has a right to marry another has the right to file for divorce.
   2. Hence, an unhappy spouse wishing to be freed, in order to marry another person:
      (a) May, by following this theory, go out and commit fornication.
      (b) Then, based on his own fornication, file for divorce.
      (c) And, be free to marry again. Of course, all of this would be with God's approval.
   3. That may seem so absurd that it is not reasonable, but it follows the same line of reason.
      (a) Following this reasoning empowers the fornicator to circumvent God's plan!
      (b) And, simultaneously, it destroys the sanctity of God's precious creation—marriage.
D. If the guilty party can remarry, then spouse-swapping and synchronized unfaithfulness would be acceptable.
   1. If a husband and wife become unhappy in their marriage, they could:
      (a) Plan and agree for both of them to have sex outside of marriage.
      (b) Then, plan and agree for both of them to put the other away for fornication.
      (c) Then, be free from each other and free to remarry at will with God's blessing.
      (d) Then, having found this "way out" of God's original plan, live happily ever after.
   2. If a husband and wife meet another couple that attracts them, they could:
      (a) Plan and agree among the four of them to swap spouses.
      (b) Make two new happy marriages out of two old unhappy marriages.
      (c) And, do all of this with Jesus' permission.
   3. Both of these scenarios could be repeated at will without limit. And without fault!
E. If the guilty party can remarry, then extremely heinous sex acts would free one to remarry.
   1. "Fornication" (Greek *porneia)* means "every kind of unlawful sexual intercourse."
   2. The word includes more than just "having an affair" (as we might define it today).
   3. Therefore, while a faithful Christian who was abused and abandoned by a spouse cannot remarry, according to the guilty-party-can-remarry doctrine:
      (a) Someone who has had sex with a person of the same gender, or sex with an animal, or sex with a relative, or sex with a child is FREED (by God) to remarry.
      (b) Regardless of civil or criminal laws of the land, if a put-away fornicator has a God-given right to remarry, then God's law (superseding man's law) would allow it.
   4. Thankfully God's Word does not permit fornicators to remarry.
      (a) Fornication is fornication!
      (b) Jesus did NOT open the door for ANY put-away fornicator to remarry!
      (c) In fact, He kept that door completely shut!
      (d) Being married to any having-been-put-away fornicator is adultery every time!
F. It is not suggested that advocates of this doctrine would teach or allow such conclusions.
   1. But, their doctrine (that a put-away fornicator can remarry) does teach and allow!
   2. This is not an attempt to be unfair to those who believe and teach this doctrine.
   3. But, it is an exercise in the exposing of a very serious and dangerous false doctrine.

V. **The Put Away-Fornicator May Not Remarry: Answering a Few Arguments That Are Made**
   A. The most common arguments made in support of this doctrine are stated in I-A and I-B, at the beginning of this chapter.
      1. Roman numeral points II, III & IV sufficiently answer those two common arguments.
      2. The following arguments are often made in response to the truths set out in II, III & IV.
      3. Short answers are offered for each one.

B. Some advocates of this doctrine have made a "handcuffed argument."
   1. The argument states, basically, that when two people marry each other that they lock themselves (figuratively) into a set of handcuffs. When one of them is unfaithful and put away, the handcuffs are removed (by God) and both are free to remarry. The thrust of their argument is that when one side of the handcuffs is loosed, both sides are, as an automatic result, freed from each other.
   2. First of all, understand that an illustration is and only can be an illustration.
      (a) Illustrations do not teach truths. Illustrations only illustrate.
      (b) They can only be properly used to illustrate truths that God has established Himself.
      (c) Therefore, even if an illustration is convincing and may seem "unanswerable":
         (1) If the illustration is illustrating a falsehood, then the illustration is powerless.
         (2) That's the problem with this "handcuffed" argument – it has NO basis of truth.
   3. To use a "handcuff illustration" properly, there would have to be three sets of cuffs.
      (a) In marriage, husband & wife are not only "handcuffed" to each other (figuratively).
      (b) Each spouse is "handcuffed" to God and the law of God.
      (c) While they may feel that they have been "unlocked from each other" in divorce, the truth is that they have not been unlocked/unbound from the law of God, until God says that they have been unlocked/unbound from His law!
      (d) Guilty parties are not free from Jesus' teachings, which require they remain single.
      (e) While one spouse may be "un-handcuffed" from his/her spouse & the law of God, it does not mean that the other spouse has been automatically "un-handcuffed."
C. Some advocates of this doctrine have argued this is condemning the guilty to a life of celibacy.
   1. It is suggested that some people cannot live without sex and this law is too strict.
   2. But, what about divorcees who are not guilty of fornication but some trivial matter?
      (a) Did not Jesus teach that they must live celibate (Matt. 19:9; 1 Cor. 7:10-11)?
      (b) If the Lord commanded such from the non-fornicators, how would it be too much to command the fornicators to live the rest of their lives without sex?
   3. If there are persons who "cannot live without sex," then:
      (a) How can we condemn rape, premarital sex, etc.? Isn't that just a natural expression of their need to fulfill something that they cannot control?
      (b) Would Jesus actually command something that is impossible for man to obey?
   4. Actually, Jesus taught that a person could choose to live without sex (cf. Mt. 19:12).
      (a) In fact, Jesus said that such a lifestyle can be "for the kingdom of heaven's sake."
      (b) Paul taught that a person could choose to live without sex (cf. 1 Cor. 7:7, 34, 40).
      (c) Both taught that such a lifestyle is possible for the sake of the kingdom.
      (d) Therefore, it is not man who is condemning to celibacy, but actually Jesus Himself.
      (e) And, with Jesus, a Christian can do all things necessary to please God (Phil. 4:13).
   5. Let us not be those who "strengthen the hands of evildoers" (Jer. 23:14).
   6. Let us remember and teach that "the way of the unfaithful is hard" (Prov. 13:15).
   7. It is also helpful to consider Hebrews 12:16-17; Matthew 12:43-45; 1 Corinthians 6:18.
D. Some advocates of this doctrine have argued that marriage is to be honorable among all.
   1. Their suggestion is that forbidding the guilty from remarriage is not honorable.
   2. However, in Hebrews 13:4, God Himself makes a clear distinction between:
      (a) Marriage that is to be held in honor and the bed undefiled, and
      (b) Those who are fornicators and adulterers.
   3. It is the fornicator who dishonors the sanctity of marriage.
   4. Marriage, God's way, is honorable! Fornicators and adulterers dishonor God's way!

VI. Souls Are at Risk When They Believe and Act upon This False Doctrine!
   A. God wanted man to understand just how serious fornication and its consequences are!
      1. The awfulness & destructiveness of this sin defies full understanding & measurement.
         (a) Taking the gift of sexual relations outside of marriage is a sin against:
            God, one's own body, one's spouse, one's children, the church & even mankind!
         (b) God singles out the sin and the one who commits the sin as the worst action that
            could ever be taken against His holy institution of marriage.
      2. God gave ONLY ONE cause for a spouse to put away his/her mate = fornication!
      3. It is the ONLY action that is so intolerable to a marriage that God permitted divorce!
      4. It is the ONE act that can make a spouse "one flesh" with a third party (1 Cor. 6:16).
      5. Therefore, it is no wonder that God removes a fornicator's right to stay married (if
         the innocent party chooses to put him/her away) or to be married to another.
   B. If a put-away fornicator could really remarry with God's 100% hearty approval:
      1. Then shouldn't we stop preaching on the sanctity of marriage?
      2. Marriage loses all sacredness if one can take sex outside of it & have no accountability.
      3. If nothing else, it creates a lower standard for today's families to live by.
   C. There are too many guilty parties who weigh their options & still choose to "take the risk."
      1. Some believe that they have approval from God.
      2. Some hope that God will understand and just be merciful.
      3. Yet, few of them ever consider that they're not only condemning their own souls,
         but also the souls of the ones with whom they enter these adulterous relationships.
   D. Individuals often ask, "But doesn't God forgive them when they repent?"
      1. The answer is, "Absolutely! Yes!"
      2. When a child of God repents, God forgives the sin and removes the guilt.
      3. However, there are still consequences for actions and sins that cannot be changed.
      4. The law to which one bound himself when married is still binding on him, unchanged.
      5. God's grace will forgive any repented sin; but God's law remains active and binding.
      6. Repentance requires more than just saying, "I'm sorry" (2 Cor. 7:9-10).
         (a) Repentance requires actual fruit that comes forth in real changes to one's life, as
            one is conformed to the will of God and not vice versa (Luke 3:7-8).
         (b) True repentance is hard!
         (c) (There will be a more in-depth study of repentance in a Chapter 8.)
   E. Roy Lanier, Jr. posed these two questions:
      1. "What will be the fate of those who may not commit these sins, but by their
         teaching encourage men to commit them?"
      2. "What will be the fate of encouragers of fornication and adultery?"

BIBLIOGRAPHY
For Chapter 6

Baird, James O. *And I Say Unto You.* Oklahoma City: B&B Bookhouse, 1981.

Connally, Andrew M. "A General Look at Some Contemporary Views of Divorce and Remarriage." *Your Marriage Can Be Great.* Ed. Thomas B. Warren. Jonesboro, AR: National Christian Press, 1978. 504-509.

Deaver, Roy. "Analysis of Matthew 19:3-12 and a Review of 'Except for Fornication.'" *The Spiritual Sword: Marriage, Divorce, Remarriage.* 6:2 (1975): 14-26.

---. "The 'Guilty Party' Is Not Free (In God's Sight) to Marry Again." *Your Marriage Can Be Great.* Ed. Thomas B. Warren. Jonesboro, AR: National Christian Press, 1978. 369-383.

Edwards, Earl. "Exegesis of Matthew 19:3-12." *Building Stronger Christian Families (1992 Freed-Hardeman University Lectureship).* Ed. Winford Claiborne. Henderson, TN: Freed-Hardeman University, 1992. 50-60.

---. "Exegesis of Matthew 19:3-9." *The Spiritual Sword: What Do the Scriptures Say About Divorce and Remarriage?* 28:4 (1997): 3-8.

---. "Key Scriptures: Matthew 19:3-12." *Marriage, Divorce, and Remarriage (1992 Spiritual Sword Lectureship).* Ed. Jim Laws. Memphis, TN: Getwell, 1992. 338-363.

Elkins, Garland. "Jesus' Teaching on Marriage, Divorce, and Remarriag." *Studies in Matthew.* Ed. Dub McClish. Denton, TX: Valid Publications, 1995. 385-410.

Jackson, Wayne. "Divorce and Civil Law." *Christian Courier.* Web. 11 Nov 2013.

---. "Divorce and the Guilty Party." *Christian Courier.* Web. 11 Nov 2013.

---. "False Ideas About Marriage." *Building Stronger Christian Families (1992 Freed-Hardeman University Lectureship).* Ed. Winford Claiborne. Henderson, TN: Freed-Hardeman University, 1992. 137-153.

---. *The Teaching of Jesus Christ on Divorce & Remarriage.* Stockton, CA: Courier Publications, 2002.

Lanier, Roy H., Jr. "Marriage, Divorce and Remarriage Discussion Forum, No. VIII: Matthew 19:9: 'The Rights of the Guilty Party.'" *Studies in 1 Corinthians.* Ed. Dub McClish. Denton, TX: Pearl Street, 1982. 469-478

Lanier, Roy H., Sr. *20 Years of the Problem Page (Vol. 1).* Abilene, TX: Quality Publications, 1984. 147-153.

McClish, Dub. "Is It the Case That the Guilty Party (in Cases of Marital Unfaithfulness) Is As Free to Marry Again As the Innocent Party?" *The Spiritual Sword: Another Look at Marriage, Divorce, Remarriage.* 19:1 (1987): 17-20.

McCord, Hugo. *Volume Two: Fifty Years of Lectures.* 433-438.

Pharr, David. "May the Guilty Party Remarry?" *Marriage, Divorce, and Remarriage (1992 Spiritual Sword Lectureship).* Ed. Jim Laws. Memphis, TN: Getwell, 1992. 450-461.

---. "Shall the Guilty Go Free?" *The Spiritual Sword: What Do the Scriptures Say About Divorce and Remarriage?* 28:4 (1997): 17-21.

Rader, Donnie V. *Marriage, Divorce and Remarriage.* Bowling Green, KY: Guardian of Truth Foundation, 2003.

Warren, Thomas B. "Some Crucial Questions on "The-Guilty-Party-Can-Remarry" Theory." *Your Marriage Can Be Great.* Ed. Thomas B. Warren. Jonesboro, AR: National Christian Press, 1978. 384-386.

---. "Some Questions on 'The Guilty Party Is Free' Theory." *The Spiritual Sword: Marriage, Divorce, Remarriage.* 6:2 (1975): 41-43.

Chapter 7: <u>Deserted Believers Are Not Free to Remarry!</u>

I. **Some Believe That If a Non-Christian Spouse Leaves a Christian Spouse, Then the Christian Is Free to Divorce and Remarry with God's Approval.**

   A. Some argue that 1 Corinthians 7:15 provides additional cause for divorce to Matthew 19:9.

      1. Since 1 Corinthians 7 came after Matthew 19, some suggest it modifies Matthew 19:9.

   B. Some argue that Matthew 19:9 is a covenant passage that only applies to Christians (i.e., a Christian married to a Christian), and that 1 Corinthians 7:12-16 is God's marriage laws for a Christian married to a non-Christian (since Matthew 19:9 doesn't apply to them).

      1. See Chapter 4 for Biblical discussion & response to Matthew 19 as a covenant passage.

      2. If this is even remotely true, then 1 Corinthians 7 is a contradiction of Matthew 19.

   C. Some argue (from 1 Cor. 7:15) that "desertion" is another cause for divorce & remarriage.

      1. They hold that a believer deserted by an unbeliever is free to remarry without adultery.

      2. This is in addition to the one exception that Jesus gave (for fornication) in Matthew 19:9.

      3. It is not a contradiction of Jesus but simply addressing a situation He did not address.

      4. This cause for divorce is often referred to as "The Pauline Privilege," denoting that the Apostle Paul was the one who stated this cause and not Jesus.

      5. This line of argumentation goes back to at least the 4th century (with Chrysostom).

      6. It is a part of "The Code of Canon Law" of the Roman Catholic Church.

      7. It has also been believed and defended by some brethren within the Lord's church.

   D. Some argue that "not under bondage" (in 1 Cor. 7:15) releases the Christian.

      1. They argue the Christian is no longer bound to the marriage but the bond is broken.

      2. Thus, if they are no longer bound to the marriage, then they are free to remarry.

   E. This line of argumentation is made from a faulty interpretation of 1 Corinthians 7:15.

      1. This line of argumentation compromises the Lord's teaching on MDR.

II. **A Brief Examination of 1 Corinthians 7:10-16.**

   A. In 1 Corinthians 7, Paul addressed about seven different questions regarding marriage.

      1. The Christians in Corinth had written to Paul to ask him some questions (7:1).

      2. As with all Biblical writings, Paul's words in response were inspired of God.

      3. While Jesus may not have specifically addressed each of these issues while on earth:

         (a) All of the questions from the Corinthians can and must be answered in light of Jesus' teaching on the subject of marriage (particularly in Matthew 5:32; 19:9).

         (b) His teachings have universal application to every marriage and divorce scenario.

   B. Instructions are given to all husbands and wives (1 Cor. 7:10-11).

      1. First of all, as Jesus taught while on earth, they are to remain married (7:10).

         (a) Marriage is for life, "till death parts" (Rom. 7:2-3; 1 Cor. 7:39).

         (b) There is only one exception, given by Jesus in Matthew 19:9.

         (c) Paul is addressing the general rule and universal principles of marriage; the context of 1 Corinthians 7 is not about remarriage or the exception.

      2. If a separation does occur, however:

         (a) They are to remain unmarried or be reconciled (7:11).

         (b) They are still considered to be married to each other—he is "her husband."

      3. Jesus, and therefore the entirety of Scripture, gives only one exception, allowing a married but sinned-against spouse to divorce and remarry (Matt. 19:9; 5:32).

C. Instructions are given to Christians who are married to unbelievers (7:12-16).
   1. This is the context in which the verse (v. 15) under controversy is found.
   2. "The rest" likely refers to the additional issues/questions asked by the brethren (7:12).
   3. Being married to a non-Christian is not justification for divorce (7:12-13).
   4. It is still a marriage joined by God and holy in His sight (7:14).
   5. Verse 15 is a parenthesis amidst verses 12-16, which provides an "exception" to the overall aim of the passage that the Christian should remain married to the unbeliever.
   6. A Christian, whose first allegiance is to Christ, is not so obligated/bound to keep the marriage together as to violate or surrender that first allegiance (7:15; cf. Acts 5:29).
   7. The Christian mate must do what is right in order to lead both to salvation (7:16).

III. **Every Part of 1 Corinthians 7 Is Equally Inspired and Authorized By God.**
   A. Some try to make something out of Paul's statements, "I say" and "not I but the Lord."
      1. Some try to make a distinction between God's commands and Paul's opinions.
   B. In the specific section of this study, the inspired apostle was distinguishing between:
      1. What the Lord taught & authorized while on earth (Matt. 5:32; 19:9), and
      2. What the Lord taught & authorized through the Holy Spirit after He left (Eph. 3:1-5).
   C. The overriding truth is that every word in 1 Corinthians 7 (and the rest of the Bible, for that matter) was chosen, inspired and authorized by God, and not Paul!
      1. The things Paul wrote were not his own opinions (cf. 2 Pet. 1:20-21).
      2. The things Paul wrote were not the teachings of other men (Gal. 1:11-12).
      3. The things Paul wrote were fully inspired (1 Cor. 2:9-13; 2 Tim. 3:16).
      4. The things Paul wrote were "the commandments of the Lord" (1 Cor. 14:37).
      5. The things Paul wrote were equally the words/authority of the Lord as those spoken by Jesus during His earthly ministry (John 16:13-15).

IV. **Desertion By a Non-Christian Spouse Is Not an Authorized Cause for Divorce & Remarriage!**
   A. To make this argument is to force something onto the text that is just not there!
   B. It is important to understand the verb "depart" (Greek *chorizo).*
      1. In the phrase, "if the unbeliever departs," it is a present middle indicative verb.
         (a) It is noting that the unbeliever himself is attempting to or desiring to depart.
      2. In the phrase, "let him depart," it is a present middle imperative verb.
         (a) The Christian may permit the separation (but it is not sanctioning it at all).
   C. As seen clearly in Chapter 6, Jesus' use of the word "except":
      1. Is a word that means "if and only if," and there's one and only one exception.
      2. In John 3:3-5 means there is one and only one way to enter the kingdom.
      3. In Matthew 19:9 means there is one and only one cause for divorce and remarriage.
      4. Must be the law under which every other passage is studied and explained.
   D. The specific context of 1 Corinthians 7:15 must be studied out and respected.
      1. A series of questions were asked to Paul by the Corinthians about the status of a marriage when one spouse becomes a Christian and the other does not.
      2. This would likely create some conflict in the marriage, including demands from the unbeliever upon the Christian to make compromises to "save" their marriage.
         (a) The unbeliever may even force the Christian to make a choice: "Christ or me!"
         (b) Is this really even an option for the Christian to renounce his faith in Christ?
         (c) If the Christian chose the unbelieving mate over Christ, that would be slavery!
         (d) The Christian is permitted to "let him depart" and not compromise loyalty to Christ.
      3. Separation is only allowed if the non-Christian forces the Christian to choose.
         (a) And, even then, divorce and remarriage are not even discussed or permitted.

E. Note carefully: "Divorce" is not even being discussed in the context of 1 Corinthians 7:15.
   1. While the context of Matthew 19 is divorce, the context of 1 Corinthians 7 is not!
   2. The word used for divorce in the Greek New Testament is *apoluo*.
      (a) See Chapter 5, where *apoluo* is defined as "to loose away, send away, dismiss."
      (b) Found in MDR passages, such as Matt. 5:31-32; 19:3-9; Mark 10:2-4, 11-12; Luke 16:18
   3. The word *apoluo* is noticeably absent in 1 Corinthians 7:10-15.
      (a) If this is a section about "divorce," why would the common word for it be absent?
   4. The word *chorizo* (the word used in 1 Cor. 7) means to "divide" or "separate."
      (a) It is a generic term, used only 12 times in the N.T., including in Matthew 19:6.
      (b) Other passages include: Acts 1:4; 18:1-2; Rom. 8:35, 29; Phile 15; Heb. 7:26.
      (c) There is no indication that it means "divorce" in 1 Corinthians 7:10, 11, 15.
      (d) The generic (and typical) meaning of "separate" is intended (and so translated).
      (e) "Departs" *(chorizo)* in 1 Corinthians 7:15 literally means "separates himself."
   5. Jesus spoke clearly and conclusively regarding divorce in Matthew 5:32 and 19:9.
      (a) If 1 Corinthians 7 even appears to contradict Jesus' clear and conclusive teaching, then 1 Corinthians 7 cannot be addressing the subject of divorce.
F. Note carefully: "Remarriage" is not being discussed in the context of 1 Corinthians 7:15.
   1. While some want the use of *chorizo* ("departs, let him depart") to imply a broken marriage bond and a right to remarry, neither the word nor the context will allow it.
   2. The same word *(chorizo)* is used in verse 11.
      (a) It is obvious that the departure/separation in verse 11 did not permit remarriage.
      (b) Therefore, there is no justification for remarriage after a departure in verse 15.
      (c) The departure *(chorizo)* was not a termination of the marriage bond.
      (d) While "divorce" has a specific meaning to us, *chorizo* is used in the N.T. with a general meaning ("separate, divide, depart").
   3. In the whole of 1 Corinthians 7, there is NO mention of remarriage until verse 39.
      (a) And, in verse 39, it is a widow whose right to remarry is under discussion.
      (b) There is no discussion of remarriage anywhere else in the context.
G. There is no divorce or second marriage in view in this passage, for:
   1. It is still calling them "husband" and "wife."
   2. There is still the possibility of a reunion.
   3. Divorce is not even mentioned and no another cause for divorce & remarriage is given.
H. If Paul had permitted divorce and remarriage in 7:15, he would have contradicted his own teaching just four verses earlier, when he taught that celibacy or reconciliation were the only two options for a spouse whose mate had departed.

V. **The Word "Bondage" in 1 Corinthians 7:15 Must Be Understood Biblically!**
   A. "Bondage" is from the Greek verb *douloo*, akin to the noun form *doulos*.
      1. The verb means "to make a slave, to enslave, to be bound as a slave."
      2. Combined, the verb and noun forms appear 135 times in the Greek New Testament.
   B. The verb "bondage" *(douloo)* is never used in the N.T. to refer to the marriage bond.
      1. The NASB translates the verb as "enslaved" frequently (cf. Acts 7:6, Tit. 2:3; 2 Pet. 2:19).
      2. It is used of the Christian being enslaved to God & to righteousness (Rom. 6:18, 22).
      3. But, marriage is never viewed in the Bible as "slavery."
      4. In passages where Paul was writing of the marriage bond (and even here in 1 Corinthians 7), he used a different word—*deo* (1 Cor. 7:27, 39; Rom. 7:2).
      5. By using a different word, readers would know this was not about the marriage bond.
      6. In 1 Corinthians 7:15, "not under bondage" is not the marriage relationship/bond.

C. If a non-Christian spouse "departs," the Lord assures the Christian that:
1. One's first allegiance is to God (Acts 5:29).
2. One is not expected to or enslaved to compromise his relationship with God in order to maintain a relationship with his spouse.
3. The Christian is not under bondage (or a slave) to relinquish his Christianity and to prevent departure or pursue (or even force) reconciliation with the departed spouse.
4. If Christians were obligated to "desert" the Lord to maintain a marriage with a "deserted" (or threatening to "desert") spouse, that would be an enslavement.
5. Still, even if a non-Christian spouse does depart, and if the Christian does "let her depart" to maintain his allegiance to God, the Christian is not permitted to remarry.
D. In 1 Corinthians 7:15, the word for "bondage," *douloo*, is in the Greek perfect tense.
1. The Greek perfect tense denotes a completed action (past) but with a present result.
(a) It emphasizes something taking place in the past but with results still abiding.
2. The perfect tense of "bondage" in 1 Corinthians 7:15 literally translates to:
(a) "He was not bound and still is not bound."
(b) "He was not enslaved (before his spouse departed and was still with him) and is not now enslaved (after the departure has happened)."
(c) The Christian has never been in the bondage that is under consideration here.
3. The word "bondage" (in the perfect tense) cannot at all refer to the marriage.
(a) The Christian was married to his spouse (and still is)—bondage cannot be marriage.
(b) If "bondage" is "marriage," then substitute the word into the sentence:
(1) "The believer was not married and still is not married."
(2) Substitution does not fit because it is not the marriage.
4. A Christian was not required to compromise his faith (when his spouse was still with him), and he is not enslaved to compromise his faith for his spouse now.
E. The Christian's bond to Christ is stronger than the bond to his unbelieving spouse.
1. The bond between a Christian & Christ is to take precedence over every other bond!
2. If a Christian favors any other bond (ex: with parent, spouse, etc.) over his bond to Christ, then he is not worthy to be considered a disciple of Christ (Luke 14:26).

VI. Matthew 19:9 and 1 Corinthians 7:15 Must Stand in Complete Harmony!
A. Jesus' teaching in Matthew 19:9 clearly applies comprehensively to ALL men ("whosoever").
B. Jesus' teaching in Matthew 19:9 was intended for the duration of the Christian age.
C. Jesus' teaching in Matthew 19:9 is based on God's original plan in Genesis 2:24.
1. God's original plan for marriage was intended for all of humanity.
2. Jesus' appeal to that original plan for marriage was intended for all of humanity.
D. Jesus' teaching in Matthew 19:9 must apply equally and fairly to all marriages.
1. If a man divorces his wife for trivial reasons, neither of them can remarry (Mt. 19:9).
2. If two Christians separate, both of them must remain unmarried (1 Cor. 7:10-11).
3. However, can a Christian deserted by a non-Christian divorce and remarry?
4. Wouldn't that make God a respecter of persons?
E. Therefore, Paul's teaching in 1 Corinthians 7 must:
1. Also apply to all of humanity.
2. Harmonize with all Biblical teaching on MDR, including Genesis 2 and Matthew 19.
3. Complement and support Jesus' teaching regarding marriage, divorce, remarriage and the one divine exception, and not contradict it!

BIBLIOGRAPHY
For Chapter 7

Baird, James O. *And I Say Unto You.* Oklahoma City: B&B Bookhouse, 1981.

Deaver, Roy. "Marriage, Divorce and Remarriage Discussion Forum, No. II: 1 Corinthians 7:15: 'Not Under Bondage.'" *Studies in 1 Corinthians.* Ed. Dub McClish. Denton, TX: Pearl Street, 1982. 375-390.

---. "Matthew 19:9 and 1 Corinthians 7." *The Spiritual Sword: Another Look at Marriage, Divorce, Remarriage.* 19:1 (1987): 6-12.

---. "Some Errors on 1 Corinthians 7 Set Forth and Refuted." *Your Marriage Can Be Great.* Ed. Thomas B. Warren. Jonesboro, AR: National Christian Press, 1978. 437-453.

Dobbs, H.A. (Buster). "Is a Christian Who Has Been Divorced By an Unbelieving Spouse Free to Remarry?" *Marriage, Divorce, and Remarriage (1992 Spiritual Sword Lectureship).* Ed. Jim Laws. Memphis, TN: Getwell, 1992. 476-486.

Elkins, Garland. "Jesus' Teaching on Marriage, Divorce, and Remarriag." *Studies in Matthew.* Ed. Dub McClish. Denton, TX: Valid Publications, 1995. 385-410.

Floyd, Harvey. "More in Review of the So-Called 'Pauline Privilege.'" *The Spiritual Sword: Marriage, Divorce, Remarriage.* 6:2 (1975): 37-39.

---. "The Doctrine of the So-Called 'Pauline Privilege' Is Seen to Be False By the Greek Text of 1 Corinthians 7:15." *Your Marriage Can Be Great.* Ed. Thomas B. Warren. Jonesboro, AR: National Christian Press, 1978. 498-503.

Jackson, Wayne. *Divorce & Remarriage (A Study Discussion).* Stockton, CA: Courier Publications, 1983.

---. "False Ideas About Marriage." *Building Stronger Christian Families (1992 Freed-Hardeman University Lectureship).* Ed. Winford Claiborne. Henderson, TN: Freed-Hardeman University, 1992. 137-153.

---. "What Is the Meaning of 'Not Under Bondage" (1 Cor. 7:15)?" *Christian Courier.* Web. 11 Nov 2013.

Lanier, Roy H., Jr. "A Look at 1 Corinthians 7:15." *The Spiritual Sword: What Do the Scriptures Say About Divorce and Remarriage?* 28:4 (1997): 12-16.

Lanier, Roy H., Sr. "Review of the Divorce Dilemma." *The Spiritual Sword: Marriage, Divorce, Remarriage.* 6:2 (1975): 30-33.

---. "A Review of 'The Divorce Dilemma.'" *Your Marriage Can Be Great.* Ed. Thomas B. Warren. Jonesboro, AR: National Christian Press, 1978. 465-485.

---. "Review of the So-Called 'Pauline Privilege.'" *The Spiritual Sword: Marriage, Divorce, Remarriage.* 6:2 (1975): 33-37.

---. "The So-Called 'Pauline Privilege' Is of Human Origin." *Your Marriage Can Be Great.* Ed. Thomas B. Warren. Jonesboro, AR: National Christian Press, 1978. 486-497.

Lipe, David L. "Answering Marriage Questions." *Perfecting God's People (2010 Freed-Hardeman University Lectureship).* Ed. David L. Lipe. Henderson, TN: Freed-Hardeman University, 2010. 74-94.

---. "1 Corinthians 7 Does Not Provide Another Ground for Divorce and Remarriage." *Your Marriage Can Be Great.* Ed. Thomas B. Warren. Jonesboro, AR: National Christian Press, 1978. 454-459.

McCord, Hugo. *Fifty Years of Lectures.* 225-226.

Miller, Dave. "A Look at 1 Corinthians 7:15." *The Spiritual Sword: Another Look at Marriage, Divorce, Remarriage.* 19:1 (1987): 44-47.

Music, Goebel. "Is It the Case That Paul (in 1 Cor. 7) Contradicted What Jesus Taught in Matthew 19:9?" *The Spiritual Sword: Another Look at Marriage, Divorce, Remarriage.* 19:1 (1987):15-17.

Pryor, Neale. "Divorce—Its Meaning." *Your Marriage Can Be Great.* Ed. Thomas B. Warren. Jonesboro, AR: National Christian Press, 1978. 98-104.

Rader, Donnie V. *Marriage, Divorce and Remarriage.* Bowling Green, KY: Guardian of Truth Foundation, 2003.

Winkler, Wendell. *Solving Problems God's Way.* Tuscaloosa, AL: Winkler Publications, 2004.

Workman, Gary. "Key Scriptures: 1 Corinthians 7:1-40." *Marriage, Divorce, and Remarriage (1992 Spiritual Sword Lectureship).* Ed. Jim Laws. Memphis, TN: Getwell, 1992. 375-416.

Chapter 8: Adulterous Marriages Are Sinful & Must Be Severed!

I. **Some Believe That Non-Christians Who Have Divorced and Remarried (for Unscriptural Reasons But in Accordance with Civil Law) May Continue, Upon Conversion, in Their Most Current Marriage (and With God's Full Approval).**

A. Essentially, non-Christians are permitted to divorce and remarry without any limits (as long as they have obeyed the civil law) before becoming Christians, and then they may (and even must) remain with the one to whom they are married when they're baptized.

B. Some insist that non-Christians are not amenable to Christ's law but to civil law only.

   1. Their claim is that marriages between non-Christians are not bound by N.T. law.

   2. Thus, if a non-Christian marriage violates N.T. laws of Christianity, there is no sin.

   3. They profess that only those in the church are accountable to Christ's marriage laws, and therefore, everyone out of the church may divorce and remarry (without limit).

   4. They are only amenable to God's marriage laws after they have been baptized.

   5. See Roman Numeral II below for a Scriptural response to this erroneous belief.

C. Some teach that Paul authorized any married non-Christian, regardless of their present marital state, to "remain in the same calling in which he was called" (1 Cor. 7:20).

   1. They teach that if someone was living in adultery when converted to Christ:

      (a) They not only are permitted and approved to stay married (without further sin),

      (b) They must now remain married to their current spouse (without further divorce).

   2. Would this not, of necessity, also include polygamists, homosexuals, etc.? How could they be exempt from this law and God's promise of salvation?

   3. See Roman Numeral III below for a Scriptural response to this erroneous belief.

D. Some assert that Christianity is not about abolishing relationships but sanctifying them, for "the unbelieving husband is sanctified by the wife..." (1 Cor. 7:14).

   1. However, this puts Jesus in the position of sanctifying activity which He condemned, without any change (or cessation) on the part of the one engaged in the activity.

   2. It wrests a meaning from the passage, which contradicts the passage and the Bible.

   3. Is a person set apart and made holy (acceptable and presentable) to Him merely for being married to a Christian? If so, what purpose does His plan of salvation have?

   4. 1 Corinthians 7:14 is not dealing with a sinful or adulterous marriage, but it is addressing a Christian who is rightfully (lawfully in God's eyes) married to a non-Christian.

      (a) The verse has to do with the continued holy nature of marriage (cf. Matt. 19:6).

      (b) The verse has to do with the purifying influence of the Word and the Christian life upon the non-Christian in the marriage, as well as on the children (cf. 1 Pet. 3:1).

E. Some argue that baptism washes away adulterous relationships.

   1. They actually believe that non-Christians are amenable to the law of Christ.

      (a) Therefore, they believe that non-Christians can and do commit adultery by not following God's design for marriage and by violating Matthew 19:9.

      (b) However, once baptized, they say a couple (once adulterous) can stay together.

   2. They reason like this: when one is baptized, all past sins are forgiven.

      (a) Included in the forgiveness is the sinful act of entering an adulterous marriage.

      (b) Consequently, after being baptized, one may continue in the marriage, for it is no longer adultery (which has been forgiven).

3. They claim that the act of baptism takes a sinful/unscriptural relationship and makes it fully acceptable/Scriptural in the eyes of God.
4. See Roman Numeral IV below for a Scriptural response to this erroneous belief.

F. Some allege adultery is among those sins that cannot be undone, and therefore, couples living in adultery should not judge any change to their relationship as an essential act.
1. They argue that, like a murderer cannot bring back someone he has murdered (that act is simply "undoable") and cannot change his relationship to the one murdered, likewise it is not essential that an adulterer force a change of relationship.
2. The murderer can "repent," "change his conduct" & "promise to never do it again."
3. In like manner, it is argued that an adulterer can simply "repent" and "promise to never divorce and remarry again." (Some will even say that Christians in unscriptural marriages can do the same thing and stay in their present marriage.)
4. In order to justify unscriptural divorces and remarriages, some are redefining "repentance" to be merely "I'm sorry" but keep on living with adulterous partner.
5. Of course, what would be expected of polygamists, homosexuals, prostitutes, etc.?
6. See Roman Numeral V below for a Scriptural response to this erroneous belief.

G. Some believe that the early church accepted into the church (almost out of necessity) those living in adultery, without consideration of their present marital status or even thought of requiring any change.
1. The practice and lifestyle of adultery was so prevalent, the church would have had no choice but to accept them (so it is claimed).
2. Of course, one must ask how the prevalence of any sin makes it justifiable.
   (a) Does the Lord become soft on sin when "everyone is doing it"?
   (b) Will/Can the same be applied to polygamy, homosexuality, pedophilia, etc.?
3. See Roman Numeral IV, C, 5 below for a Scriptural response to this erroneous belief.

H. Some cannot accept that any marriage must be dissolved when children are present.
1. When heartstrings are tugged, marriage laws must be pliable and yield.
2. However, would that not also be true of all of God's other laws?
3. And, would this not apply equally to marriages in the church & outside the church?
4. See Roman Numeral VI, A below for a Scriptural response to this matter.

I. As we consider what Scripture teaches about this matter, we must remember:
1. Our personal beliefs and feelings have no place in determining what God authorizes.
2. One passage of God's Word will not ever contradict another passage of God's Word.
3. If we have an interpretation of one passage that contradicts another passage:
   (a) Our interpretation is wrong (not God's Word),
   (b) And our interpretation must be changed (not God's Word)!

II. All Mankind Is Amenable/Answerable to the Law of God, Including Non-Christians!

A. This point is considered and addressed in Chapter 4, as well.
B. The prevalence of divorce & remarriage in our society has been difficult on the church:
1. In evangelism, should we teach prospects the whole truth about MDR?
2. In evangelism, should we emphasize the corrective action that repentance requires?
3. Or, in evangelism, should we relax God's MDR standards to comply with modernity?
4. Additionally, when members of the church move in from other places:
   (a) Should shepherds be concerned if sheep are living in adultery?
   (b) Or, should shepherds just mind their business and not create waves?

C. Unfortunately, many brethren have sought to ease God's plan for non-Christians.
  1. They have tried to affirm that God's marriage law does not apply to non-Christians.
  2. Therefore, before becoming a Christian, unbelievers can divorce and remarry freely.
    (a) It does not matter for what reasons they had divorced prior to conversion.
    (b) None of their previous divorces and remarriages will "count against them."
    (c) Upon conversion, it will be as if their current marriage was their first marriage.
D. The truth is that all mankind is answerable to God's law on marriage!
  1. In Matthew 19, Jesus restored marriage to God's original plan (from the beginning).
    (a) God's original plan was applicable to all mankind.
    (b) There were no Jews or Gentiles in the beginning...just God's first marriage.
    (c) There were no Christians or non-Christians in the beginning...just God's creation.
    (d) It applied to all at the beginning; Jesus restored its universal application in Mt. 19.
    (e) Therefore, God's marriage laws apply to the entire human race, as He intended.
  2. Jesus directed His marital instructions to "whoever" (Mt. 19:9) and "everyone" (5:32).
    (a) The Lord intentionally chose words that would emphasize universal application.
    (b) The church had not yet been established, yet He was giving laws for life within it.
    (c) Why would Jesus deliver His marriage law to Jews if it did not apply to them also?
    (d) In the first century, Jesus' marriage laws applied to those people **before** they became Christians (Matt. 19) and **after** they had become Christians (1 Cor. 7.).
    (e) How could anyone believe that it would be any different today?
    (f) The Lord's marriage laws apply to ALL people – "whoevers" and "everyones"!
E. All mankind can violate God's law on marriage, therefore, all are answerable!
  1. In all three dispensations (Patriarchal, Mosaic & Christian):
    (a) God has had marriage laws.
    (b) It has been possible for individuals to violate those laws.
    (c) Violating the marriage vow was called "adultery" (Job 24:15; Ex. 20:14; Mt. 19:9).
  2. By definition, the sin of adultery is a sexual act:
    (a) That involves a married person having sexual intercourse with a third party.
    (b) From the Greek *moicheia*, "unlawful intercourse with the spouse of another."
    (c) Thus, the word itself necessitates that one is violating his/her marriage vow.
    (d) There can be no "adultery" where there is no "marriage" that is violated!
  3. If one is not amenable to a law, then it is not possible for him to violate that law.
    (a) If a non-Christian is not bound by God's marriage laws, then he cannot break them (i.e., a non-Christian could not possibly commit adultery).
    (b) However, Scripture clearly reveals non-Christians who were guilty of adultery.
    (c) In 1 Corinthians 6:9-10, Paul listed numerous sinful acts, including adulterers.
    (d) Then Paul says, "And such were some of you" (6:11).
    (e) How could these Christians possibly be adulterers before they were sanctified by God, if God's laws of marriage (and therefore God's laws of consequences) did not apply to them?
    (f) The clear answer is that these unbelievers were answerable to God's marriage laws before they became Christians!
F. If God's marriage laws do not apply to non-Christian marriages, and if they can divorce and remarry as often as they like before becoming Christians (for God does not recognize their pre-conversion-to-Christ marriages as falling under His law):
  1. Wouldn't the couple need to be married "again" to each other the same day they get baptized, so that God will recognize their conversion and their marriage?

2. What happens if one of them is baptized and the other is not? Could the non-Christian still freely divorce and remarry at will, without committing sin? Would the Christian then just be stuck, and not be able to divorce/remarry like his non-Christian spouse?

3. How could the Bible possibly state that "God judges those outside" (1 Cor. 5:13), including "the sexually immoral of this world" (5:10), if God doesn't recognize, judge or even condemn their marriages?

4. This would also confuse the issue when a put-away Christian marries a non-Christian.
   (a) Jesus taught that "whoever marries her who is divorced commits adultery" (19:9).
   (b) But, what if a Christian spouse, who is put away for a non-fornication reason, marries a non-Christian?
      (1) Is a non-Christian amenable to marrying a "having-been-put-away" person?
      (2) In this scenario, does the non-Christian commit adultery or not?
      (3) Does the Christian (who was put away for non-fornication) commit adultery?
      (4) Can one of the marriage partners be committing adultery and the other not?

G. The reality is that non-Christians are (and must be) amenable to the law of Christ, otherwise they would never sin and would never need the gospel!

1. "All have sinned and fall short of the glory of God" (Rom. 3:23). "All" means "all"!
   (a) "...Sin is lawlessness" (1 John 3:4).
   (b) Therefore, since all sin, and since sin is lawlessness, all must be amenable to the law; otherwise, they'd never become a sinner (in need of the gospel) in the first place!

2. In the Great Commission, Jesus sent Christians to all non-Christians (every creature) to preach the entirety of the gospel, a message to which they're amenable and must obey (Matt. 28:18-20; Mark 16:15-16). Does Christ have "all authority" or not?

3. Jesus plainly announced that all would be judged by His Words/covenant (Jn. 12:48).
   (a) Would the Just Judge judge a person by a law to which he was not amenable?

4. Jesus is not merely "the Lord of Christians," but "He is Lord of all" (Acts 10:36).
   (a) Just because someone does not agree with that does not make it any less true.
   (b) Just because someone doesn't want to live under Him doesn't dethrone Him!

5. If a non-Christian is not amenable to God's marriage laws, then he would not be amenable to any of God's laws (cf. James 2:10; Gal. 5:3).
   (a) If he is not amenable to God's laws:
      (1) Then it would not be sinful for him to reject those laws.
      (2) Then he actually could not obey God's laws, for one cannot obey a law to which he is not amenable.
      (3) Then his standard has become civil law and anything that civil law allows.
   (b) If a person is accountable to the "plan of salvation" part of the law, then he is also accountable to the rest of the law!
   (c) Essentially, in this theory, they let civil law (and obedience to it) trump divine law.

III. God Does Not Permit a Sinner to Abide in a Sinful Relationship/Activity Upon Conversion!
A. Think about the ramifications of this position for a moment:
1. They hold that God accepts an adulterer as an adulterer who can stay in their marriage.
2. Can a non-Christian "abide/remain in whatever state" he is when he is called?
3. If he can, what is the purpose in becoming a Christian?
4. Why does he need to become a Christian?
5. What's wrong with what he's doing, if he doesn't need to change what he's doing?

B. Advocates of this position "base" their belief on words from 1 Corinthians 7:17-24.
   1. "...as the Lord has called each one, so let him walk...{20} Let each one remain in the same calling in which he was called...{24} Brethren, let each one remain with God in that state in which he was called."
   2. Their position nullifies any need to repent (see Roman Numeral V below).
C. As with all Scripture, the verses of 1 Corinthians 7 must be kept in their context!
   1. In the overall context of the entire Scripture, how could anyone believe that remaining in a sinful state (but "still converted") would ever be permissible to God?
   2. In the remote context of this chapter, there was a "present distress" (a period of hardship and persecution) that was flavoring and penetrating Paul's words (7:26).
      (a) "Because of the present distress, it is good for a man to remain as he is."
      (b) Especially in his relationships – single, married, etc. (Not dealing with sinful!)
   3. Look at the immediate context of these verses:
      (a) Paul stated a general principle for Christians to remain (unchanged) in one's life situation when converted (as long as that situation was not sinful) and to walk the Christian life in a manner worthy of and pleasing to the Lord (7:17).
      (b) To illustrate this for marriage, Paul referred to two cultural arrangements/ relationships that were not inherently sinful and need not be interrupted:
         (1) A racial one: circumcision (whether circumcised or not when called)
         (2) A social one: slavery (whether a slave or not when called)
      (c) When one became a Christian, it did not matter (to salvation purposes) if he was circumcised or not! Either way, just remain the way you were when called (7:18-20).
      (d) When one became a Christian, it did not matter (to salvation purposes) if he was a slave or free! Either way, just peacefully abide in the state in which called (7:21-24).
         (1) A slave becoming a Christian had no right to shun his slave responsibility & status.
         (2) Baptism didn't change Onesimus' runaway status or responsibilities (Phile. 10-16).
      (e) Due to the big picture and the "present distress," there was no need to alter their lawful statuses, assuming such were not sinful in God's eyes!
      (f) Therefore, when one became a Christian, it did not matter (to salvation) if he was married or single, married to a Christian or married to a non-Christian! In any case, it was better to remain in the state in which called. (This had nothing to do with any sinful/unlawful relationships or marriages. Keep it in context.)
      (g) All of these matters were moral/honorable in and of themselves; none of these relationships/conditions were sinful before baptism. For the "abide-in-your-adulterous-marriage-when-called" doctrine to be valid, then all of these would equally need to be immoral (like adultery). *The context will not allow it!*
   4. In ALL circumstances, it was not the racial or social status that mattered. What mattered then and matters now is "keeping the commandments of God" (7:19)!
D. Follow this "abide-as-you-were-called" position out to its logical absurdity!
   1. If an adulterer who becomes a Christian can remain (with God's approval) married:
      (a) What about a homosexual who is married to his/her homosexual partner?
      (b) What about the polygamist who has multiple marriage partners?
      (c) What about the pimp, the drug dealer, the human trafficker, the thief, etc.?
      (d) Could any or all of these not also remain in the state in which they were called?
   2. Obviously, God was not permitting sinful relationships to remain after conversion!

IV. God Does Not Sanctify an Adulterous Relationship Upon One's Baptism!

A. The Bible clearly and repeatedly teaches that baptism washes away sins (Ac. 22:16; 2:38).
1. The blood of Jesus most definitely removes one's sins from his account (Rev. 1:5).
2. A penitent believer is baptized into the death of Jesus where His blood cleanses from all sins (Rom. 6:3-4; Acts 22:16; Eph. 5:26).

B. The Bible clearly teaches that baptism will wash away the sin of adultery (1 Cor. 6:9-11).
1. Some of the Christians in Corinth had previously been adulterers (6:9-11).
2. "But you were washed, but you were sanctified, but you were justified in the name of the Lord Jesus and by the Spirit of our God" (6:11).
3. Upon baptism into Christ, the guilt of their adultery was remitted by Jesus' blood.

C. However, there is NO PLACE in Scripture that teaches the adulterous relationship itself has been made pure, holy and acceptable in the eyes of God (and could be maintained)!
1. Advocates of this doctrine want others to believe that Christianity takes an adulterous marriage and sanctifies it to be a perfectly acceptable marriage.
2. It is interesting that advocates of this doctrine:
   (a) Clearly believe that baptism is for the remission of sins.
   (b) Clearly believe that the non-Christians were committing/living in adultery.
   (c) Clearly believe that the adulterous marriage prevented the couple from being right in the eyes of God.
   (d) Clearly believe that something had to change (with regard to the marriage), in order for God to (1) accept them as His children and (2) recognize the marriage.
3. However, baptism will not, does not and can not change:
   (a) A sinful or unlawful practice into a righteous or lawful one, or
   (b) A sinful relationship into a righteous one.
   (c) Baptism is not some kind of magic potion that resolves and resets adulterous marriages into non-adulterous marriages.
4. If a once-adulterer, washed in baptism, is permitted to continue the same marriage:
   (a) Would a once-idolater be permitted to continue worshipping idols after baptism?
   (b) Would a once-homosexual be permitted to continue homosexuality after baptism?
   (c) Would a once-thief be permitted to continue his life of stealing after baptism?
   (d) Would a once-drunkard be permitted to continue getting drunk after baptism?
   (e) Obviously, those in 1 Corinthians 6:9-11 stopped their sinful practices! Baptism cleansed them from the guilt of their sin, but only after they stopped practicing it!

D. The definition of "adultery" must be understood and applied, as it is used in Scripture.
1. Jesus clearly taught about adultery in Matthew 19:9.
   (a) "Whoever divorces his wife...and marries another, commits adultery..."
   (b) "Whoever marries her who is divorced commits adultery."
   (c) By definition, adultery is "unlawful intercourse with the spouse of another."
   (d) Adultery involves a married person having sexual intercourse with a third party.
2. "Commits adultery" is in the Greek present tense, which denotes continuous action.
   (a) The adultery is not a "one-time" act (at the wedding ceremony) and that's it.
   (b) One who divorces and marries "keeps on committing adultery."
   (c) The second marriage is continuous adultery every time they are intimate, because one (or both) of them is still married to another person (in God's eyes).
   (d) Jesus emphasized, by use of the present tense, the permanent nature of marriage.

3. Emphasizing marriage's permanent nature emphasized the ongoing nature of adultery.
    (a) To avoid adultery there are two options: celibacy or reconciliation (1 Cor. 7:10-11).
    (b) It is possible for one to "live in adultery" for the rest of one's life.
    (c) "Such **were** some of you" in 1 Corinthians 6:11 is a Greek imperfect tense.
        (1) The imperfect tense emphasizes a continuous lifestyle in the past.
        (2) It was not a single act they had committed in the past.
        (3) Adulterers were involved in an ongoing sinful lifestyle/relationship.
    (d) "You **lived** in them" in Colossians 3:7 is a Greek imperfect tense.
        (1) "Them" in verse 7 points back to the carnal behaviors in verse 5.
        (2) They had "lived in...fornication," which is all illicit sex, including adultery.
        (3) This was a continuous sin, for God still viewed the first marriage as binding.
    (e) Adultery, as defined by God, is an ongoing act that is continually violating God's will.
4. Those who commit adultery are doing so because God has/had not joined them.
    (a) Proper marriages of two eligible (in the sight of God) persons are joined by God.
    (b) Even non-Christians are joined by God in marriage (for it is a divine institution).
    (c) The Bible does NOT teach that God joins two adulterers together when baptized.
E. Baptism does change relationships, but not the marriage relationship!
    1. When a person is baptized, he is still married...and still married to the same person.
        (a) If he had no right to be in a relationship before baptism, he has no new right.
        (b) The relationship is exactly the same as it was before he was baptized.
    2. Baptism changes one's relationship with the Godhead (Mt. 28:19), but not marriage.
    3. Baptism changes one's relationship with the church (1 Cor. 12:13), but not marriage.
    4. Baptism changes one's relationship with Christ's death (Rom. 6:3), but not marriage.
    5. Jesus gave one exception for divorce and remarriage, and baptism was not it!
F. Sex that is unlawful before baptism is still unlawful sex after baptism.
    1. Premarital sex before baptism is sinful, and it remains sinful after baptism.
    2. Homosexual sex before baptism is sinful, and it remains sinful after baptism.
    3. Polygamous sex before baptism is sinful, and it remains sinful after baptism.
    4. Pedophilia sex before baptism is sinful, and it remains sinful after baptism.
    5. Incestuous sex before baptism is sinful, and it remains sinful after baptism.
    6. Bestiality sex before baptism is sinful, and it remains sinful after baptism.
    7. Prostitution sex before baptism is sinful, and it remains sinful after baptism.
    8. Likewise, adultery sex before baptism is sinful, and it remains sinful after baptism.
    9. Baptism does not sanctify any of these unauthorized sexual lifestyles!
G. Can baptism make an adulterous marriage only "half adulterous"?
    1. If only one spouse in an adulterous marriage is baptized, what does that mean?
        (a) Is one half of that marriage now living "out of adultery" and no longer sinning,
        (b) While the other half is still living "in adultery" and still in a sinful relationship?
    2. If one half of an adulterous marriage is baptized and is no longer an adulterer
       (though still living with and having sex with one to whom God did not join him/her),
        (a) Couldn't the same reasoning be used to justify one half of a homosexual,
            polygamous, pedophilic, incestuous marriage being sin-free in the eyes of God?
        (b) If not, why not? It is exactly the same from a Scriptural standpoint!
    3. Baptism does not sanctify one half or one whole of any sinful sexual lifestyle!

4. This would also confuse the issue when a put-away Christian marries a non-Christian.
    (a) Jesus taught that "whoever marries her who is divorced commits adultery."
    (b) If the put-away Christian spouse remarries, he will be committing adultery.
        (1) But what if he remarries a non-Christian? Is there adultery? For who?
        (2) What if the non-Christian is later baptized? Is the non-Christian forgiven of all adulterous activity by virtue of his baptism? What about the Christian? Is the Christian still committing adultery, but the newly baptized Christian is not?

H. Too bad John the Immerser didn't know "baptism sanctifies adulterous relationships."
  1. John the Immerser spent his last days repeatedly telling Herod that he was sinning.
    (a) "John had been saying [imperfect tense, continuous action in the past] to Herod..."
    (b) "'It is not lawful...'" [present tense, "it is and keeps on being unlawful"]
    (c) "'...For you to have...'" [present tense, "to have and to keep on having her"]
  2. John's repeated message regarding God's universal law cost him his head (his life).
  3. If only John would have told Herod and Herodias:
    (a) "While your marriage is not lawful right now, because it is adultery..."
    (b) "Just be baptized and it will be sanctified by God and you can stay together."
    (c) Shouldn't the forerunner of Jesus have known that Jesus would allow this?
  4. John did not offer that as a possibility because such a teaching is not from God!

I. Baptism washes away sins, but it doesn't wash away previous husbands or wives!

V. God Requires Genuine Repentance Before One Is Saved from Sins!

A. Repentance of sin is an absolute requirement in order to be forgiven of sin!
  1. It is a requirement of non-Christians outside of Christ (Acts 2:38; 17:30-31).
  2. It is a continued requirement of Christians who are in Christ (Acts 8:22; Rev. 2:5).

B. Baptism is completely ineffective and invalid unless preceded by genuine repentance!
  1. In Acts 2, sinners were directed, "Repent and...be baptized...for the remission..." (38).
  2. "John came...preaching a baptism of repentance for the remission of sins" (Mk. 1:4).

C. "Repentance" must be defined accurately and not popularly or socially!
  1. Repentance is often paralleled (in the mind of men) with regret or sorrow.
    (a) Some equate saying, "I'm sorry," with repentance.
    (b) Some have limited repentance to purely a mental act and nothing more.
    (c) However, regret or sorrow or just changing one's mind is not repentance!
  2. The noun "repentance" (Greek *metanoia*) and the verb "repent" (Greek *metanoeo*) are found about 60 times combined in the Greek New Testament.
    (a) The two words always carry the emphasis of:
        (1) A change of mind
        (2) That involves a change of conduct
        (3) Ultimately fulfilled in the ceasing of the past sin
  3. It involves a "change of mind" to the point of "turning about, conversion" (BDAG).
    (a) "To change one's mind or purpose"; always of "repentance" from sin (Vine).
    (b) "Referring exclusively to 'turning from one's sin'" (Renn 810)
    (c) "This change of mind involves both a turning from sin and a turning to God" (Vine).
  4. "Both noun and verb denote a radical, moral turn of the whole person from sin and to God" (Mounce 580)

(a) "Used almost exclusively for the attitude of unbelievers and sinners returning to God...urging 'conversion' to Christianity. There is no longer any question of distinguishing between change of thoughts, of heart, of actions. The change is that of the soul, of the whole person (the new creature)" (Spicq 475).

(b) "Not just any regret or repudiation but affliction, 'remorse' that inspires a desire to make reparation, even expiation" (Spicq 476).

D. "Repentance" must be defined Biblically and not popularly or socially!
1. Repentance involves more than being pricked in the heart (i.e., emotion) (Ac. 2:37-38).
2. Repentance involves more than having godly sorrow (2 Cor. 7:10).
3. Repentance involves more than acknowledging wrongdoing to God (Psa. 51:1-19).
4. Repentance involves a change of mind and a change of action (Matt. 21:28-29).
5. Repentance involves a turning from evil ways (Matt. 12:41; Jonah 3:10).
6. Repentance involves a "burning" of sinful practices & elements thereof (Ac. 19:19).
7. Repentance involves a reformed lifestyle (Luke 3:8).
8. Repentance involves fruit that is "in keeping with repentance" (Matt. 3:8).
   (a) The fruit the Lord is looking for is a reformed life that forsakes all wrongs.
9. Therefore, defined Biblically, repentance is BETWEEN the emotional conviction of godly sorrow and the ultimate changed life resulting from repentance.
   (a) Repentance is only possible when one loves the Lord so much that he wants to do His will rather than his own.
   (b) Godly sorrow leads to and produces repentance.
   (c) Repentance leads to and produces an amended life.
   (d) If one stays in an adulterous relationship, where is the amended life?
E. Repentance requires change, separation and cessation!
1. When one genuinely repents of sin, then he will cease that sinful activity in his life.
2. When one does not genuinely repent, then he will continue that sinful activity in life.
3. The key to repentance is the cessation of sinful activity!
4. Repenting of an adulterous marriage is more than just regretting a past decision and determining (and promising) to never do it again.
5. Repenting of an adulterous marriage requires a cessation of that which is sinful—i.e., a cessation of the adulterous marriage.
6. Genuine repentance has not occurred if one continues to live in adultery after baptism.
7. Genuine repentance is a cessation of sinful activity that will "sin no more" (Jn. 8:11).
8. Changing one's relationship to Christ changes everything else, esp. sinful things.
9. Baptism has no power to wash away sins until (or before) those sins are stopped!
F. Repentance demands the severing of all relationships that are in violation of God's will.
1. A prostitute, a polygamist, a homosexual, a pedophile must sever all relationships that are in violation of God's will.
2. Since this is abundantly clear, an adulterer must sever his adulterous relationship.
3. This is what John the Immerser called upon Herod to do – It is not lawful to have her!
   (a) In other words, you need to stop living according to your standards.
   (b) You need to start living according to God's standards.
   (c) As a result, you must sever every relationship that defies God's laws!
4. Wendell Winkler masterfully illustrated it this way: "If a man stole a car from your driveway, a suit from your closet, a watch from your jewelry box and ran off with your wife, what would he have to do if he genuinely repented? Would he have to return all the stolen merchandise; but, be able to keep your wife?"

G. Many will argue that it is not fair to teach that a married couple must sever their relationship, especially when children are involved.
1. To make an appeal to human rational (what is "fair") or to an emotional heart-string element (like "the children") is to concede that there is no Biblical foundation or Scriptural support for their position, and so they must go "outside" Scripture for help.
2. Even so, God did not leave us without instruction in this matter.
3. The work of Ezra was restoration—to get God's people back to following God's law.
    (a) In Ezra's day, God's people had forsaken His commandments (Ezra 9:1-15).
        (1) They had married persons whom God had forbidden them to marry.
        (2) Thus, they had sinned against God and were subject to His punishment.
    (b) In order to make things right with God, remove sin and be restored back to God:
        (1) They first recognized the seriousness of their sin (9:6-7, 14; 10:9).
        (2) They were commanded to put away their unlawful wives (10:3, 11).
        (3) They immediately followed procedure to "put away their wives" (10:11-10).
        (4) Their names are even listed at the end of the chapter to note the seriousness.
    (c) In the midst of this restoration of righteousness & repentance from wrongdoing:
        (1) There were children "who had been born to them" (10:3).
        (2) These children were also "put away" (10:3) and made "separate" (10:11).
        (3) For added emphasis, the last 3 words of the book, "they had children" (10:44).
4. Human rational and emotions should not prevent any of us from doing what is right!
    (a) Children must be cared for, and parents must fulfill their God-given roles.
    (b) However, children do not change what God says about marriage and divorce.
5. Shouldn't Christians want their children to see obedience to Christ as a priority?
6. It is possible to exercise genuine repentance, sever an adulterous marriage and still provide a home and family for children! With effort, love and prayer, we "can do all things through Christ who strengthens" (Phil. 4:13).
    (a) Would it be required of a polygamous marriage? Obviously it would!
    (b) And, if multiple marriages can be severed and the children still cared for and provided a home/family, then it can even more easily be done in just one marriage.
H. When it comes to genuine and proper repentance, why would anyone want to play it close, cut corners or argue with God's expectations for true repentance?
1. Jesus laid it out plainly in Luke 13:3 and again in Luke 13:5 –
    (a) "I tell you, no; but unless you repent you will all likewise perish."
    (b) "I tell you, no; but unless you repent you will all likewise perish."
2. God's Word clearly defines and demands genuine repentance. No human rational can change that, soften that or eliminate that!

VI. God's Marriage Laws Are Admittedly Strict and Rightfully So!

A. The disciples in Matthew 19 immediately recognized the serious and restrictive nature of God's marriage laws as He designed them and as Jesus required them to be kept.

   1. Their immediate conclusion of a life of celibacy (Matt. 19:10) shows that they understood the real binding nature (on all men) of Jesus' words regarding marriage.

   2. Jesus did not soften His teaching due to their response, but He clarified that celibacy was not God's desire and that not all men could abide by such a law (Matt. 19:11).

   3. Jesus identified only three classes of people who could live a celibate life (19:12):

     (a) Those born eunuchs (physically impotent, incapable of sexual relations)

     (b) Those made eunuchs by men (by cruelty of men)

       (1) These first two groups are physically incapable of sexual activity.

       (2) These first two groups are not fit for marriage and better off living single.

     (c) Those who have made themselves eunuchs for the kingdom of heaven's sake

       (1) These are not eunuchs because of a physical condition.

       (2) These are eunuchs by personal choice and for a spiritual reason.

       (3) These are able to devote more time and effort to the Lord and His church.

       (4) These may be some who do not have a right to remarry.

       (5) These may include a husband/wife, living in an adulterous marriage relationship, who set aside their own sexual drives and desires and put the Lord and His will first in their lives, making whatever sacrifices are necessary to be right in His eyes. It may be hard, but Jesus said "strait is the way"! There are some things (yea, many!) that are just more important and more precious than physical relationships!

B. Understanding the divine basis for marriage can help us understand God's strictness. (The remaining points of this chapter are from Wayne Jackson's 2002 book.)

   1. First of all, marriage is the most intimate of all human relationships.

     (a) Because of this, at atmosphere is created which accommodates human vulnerability.

     (b) When martial unions are treated casually, the victims of psychological trauma become numerous.

   2. Second, children have the right to grow up in a stable family relationship.

     (a) Children do not need to be shuttled from one environment to another.

       (1) That is not healthy.

     (b) A strict marriage code is doubtless designed to protect our little ones.

   3. Third, the family relationship is the cement that contributes to the cohesiveness of society.

     (a) In this connection, it helps to create the kind of tranquil atmosphere which facilitate the propagation of the gospel of Christ.

     (b) A firm marriage law is a significant contributor to Heaven's redemptive plan!

   4. When one reflects upon matters of this nature:

     (a) It is not so difficult to understand why the Lord gave marriage regulations which appear strict,

     (b) But which, upon closer consideration, really make sense.

BIBLIOGRAPHY
For Chapter 8

Baird, James O. *And I Say Unto You.* Oklahoma City: B&B Bookhouse, 1981.

(BDAG) Bauer, Walter, F.W. Danker, William F. Arndt, and F. Wilber Gingrich. *A Greek-English Lexicon of the New Testament and Other Early Christian Literature*. 3rd edition. Chicago: University of Chicago Press, 2000.

Connally, Andrew M. "A General Look at Some Contemporary Views of Divorce and Remarriage." *Your Marriage Can Be Great.* Ed. Thomas B. Warren. Jonesboro, AR: National Christian Press, 1978. 504-509.

Deaver, Roy. "Is the Non-Christian Amenable to Christ's Law of Marriage, Divorce, and Remarriage?" *Marriage, Divorce, and Remarriage (1992 Spiritual Sword Lectureship).* Ed. Jim Laws. Memphis, TN: Getwell, 1992. 487-507.

---. "Matthew 19:9 and 1 Corinthians 7." *The Spiritual Sword: Another Look at Marriage, Divorce, Remarriage.* 19:1 (1987): 6-12.

---. "Some Errors on 1 Corinthians 7 Set Forth and Refuted." *Your Marriage Can Be Great.* Ed. Thomas B. Warren. Jonesboro, AR: National Christian Press, 1978. 437-453.

Deffenbaugh, Don. "Does Baptism into Christ for the Remission of Sins Wash Away Adulterous Marriage?" *Marriage, Divorce, and Remarriage (1992 Spiritual Sword Lectureship).* Ed. Jim Laws. Memphis, TN: Getwell, 1992. 508-519.

Duncan, Bobby. "Does Baptism Sanctify an Unscriptural Relationship?" *The Spiritual Sword: What Do the Scriptures Say About Divorce and Remarriage?* 28:4 (1997): 40-43.

Eaves, Thomas F. "Jesus' Standard for Divorce and Remarriage Is the Highest One." *Your Marriage Can Be Great.* Ed. Thomas B. Warren. Jonesboro, AR: National Christian Press, 1978. 350-352.

Edwards, Earl. "Exegesis of Matthew 19:3-12." *Building Stronger Christian Families (1992 Freed-Hardeman University Lectureship).* Ed. Winford Claiborne. Henderson, TN: Freed-Hardeman University, 1992. 50-60.

---. "Exegesis of Matthew 19:3-9." *The Spiritual Sword: What Do the Scriptures Say About Divorce and Remarriage?* 28:4 (1997): 3-8.

---. "Key Scriptures: Matthew 19:3-12." *Marriage, Divorce, and Remarriage (1992 Spiritual Sword Lectureship).* Ed. Jim Laws. Memphis, TN: Getwell, 1992. 338-363.

Elkins, Garland. "Is It the Case That Repentance Demands Only Saying, 'I'm Sorry'?" *The Spiritual Sword: Another Look at Marriage, Divorce, Remarriage.* 19:1 (1987): 20-22.

---. "Jesus' Teaching on Marriage, Divorce, and Remarriag." *Studies in Matthew.* Ed. Dub McClish. Denton, TX: Valid Publications, 1995. 385-410.

---. "Let None Deal Treacherously Against the Wife of His Youth." *Your Marriage Can Be Great.* Ed. Thomas B. Warren. Jonesboro, AR: National Christian Press, 1978. 148-150.

Floyd, Harvey. "More in Review of the So-Called 'Pauline Privilege.'" *The Spiritual Sword: Marriage, Divorce, Remarriage.* 6:2 (1975): 37-39.

---. "The Doctrine of the So-Called 'Pauline Privilege' Is Seen to Be False By the Greek Text of 1 Corinthians 7:15." *Your Marriage Can Be Great.* Ed. Thomas B. Warren. Jonesboro, AR: National Christian Press, 1978. 498-503.

Hawk, Ray. "What If There Are Children (In An Adulterous Marriage)?" *Your Marriage Can Be Great.* Ed. Thomas B. Warren. Jonesboro, AR: National Christian Press, 1978. 605-609.

Jackson, Wayne. "Divorce and Civil Law." *Christian Courier.* Web. 11 Nov 2013.

---. *Divorce & Remarriage (A Study Discussion).* Stockton, CA: Courier Publications, 1983.

---. "False Ideas About Marriage." *Building Stronger Christian Families (1992 Freed-Hardeman University Lectureship).* Ed. Winford Claiborne. Henderson, TN: Freed-Hardeman University, 1992. 137-153.

---. *The Teaching of Jesus Christ on Divorce & Remarriage.* Stockton, CA: Courier Publications, 2002.

Lanier, Roy H., Jr. "Marriage, Divorce and Remarriage Discussion Forum, No. IV: 1 Corinthians 7:17-14: 'Abide in That Calling.'" *Studies in 1 Corinthians.* Ed. Dub McClish. Denton, TX: Pearl Street, 1982. 402-414.

Lanier, Roy H., Sr. "A Review of 'The Divorce Dilemma.'" *Your Marriage Can Be Great.* Ed. Thomas B. Warren. Jonesboro, AR: National Christian Press, 1978. 465-485.

---. "Review of the Divorce Dilemma." *The Spiritual Sword: Marriage, Divorce, Remarriage.* 6:2 (1975): 30-33.

---. "Review of the So-Called 'Pauline Privilege.'" *The Spiritual Sword: Marriage, Divorce, Remarriage.* 6:2 (1975): 33-37.

---. "The So-Called 'Pauline Privilege' Is of Human Origin." *Your Marriage Can Be Great.* Ed. Thomas B. Warren. Jonesboro, AR: National Christian Press, 1978. 486-497.

Lipe, David L. "Answering Marriage Questions." *Perfecting God's People (2010 Freed-Hardeman University Lectureship).* Ed. David L. Lipe. Henderson, TN: Freed-Hardeman University, 2010. 74-94.

---. "1 Corinthians 7 Does Not Provide Another Ground for Divorce and Remarriage." *Your Marriage Can Be Great.* Ed. Thomas B. Warren. Jonesboro, AR: National Christian Press, 1978. 454-459.

McClish, Dub. "Is Matthew 19:9 A Part of the Law of Christ?" *The Spiritual Sword: What Do the Scriptures Say About Divorce and Remarriage?* 28:4 (1997): 32-37.

McCord, Hugo. *Fifty Years of Lectures.* 223-224.

McGee, Pat. "A Refutation of the View That It Is Impossible to 'Live in Adultery.'" *Your Marriage Can Be Great.* Ed. Thomas B. Warren. Jonesboro, AR: National Christian Press, 1978. 510-514.

Miller, Dave. "The Biblical Doctrine of 'Repentance.'" *Marriage, Divorce, and Remarriage (1992 Spiritual Sword Lectureship).* Ed. Jim Laws. Memphis, TN: Getwell, 1992. 281-294.

Moffitt, Jerry. "Are All Men Amenable to Christ's Law?" *The Spiritual Sword: What Do the Scriptures Say About Divorce and Remarriage?* 28:4 (1997): 37-40.

---. "Is It the Case That Christianity Sanctifies Existing Relationships Even When Those Relationships Violate New Testament Teaching?" *The Spiritual Sword: Another Look at Marriage, Divorce, Remarriage.* 19:1 (1987): 28-29.

Mounce, William D. *Mounce's Complete Expository Dictionary of Old & New Testament Words.* Grand Rapids: Zondervan, 2006.

Rader, Donnie V. *Marriage, Divorce and Remarriage.* Bowling Green, KY: Guardian of Truth Foundation, 2003.

Ramsey, Johnny. "Why People in Unscriptural Marriages Must Separate." *Your Marriage Can Be Great.* Ed. Thomas B. Warren. Jonesboro, AR: National Christian Press, 1978. 557-562.

Renn, Stephen D. *Expository Dictionary of Bible Words.* Peabody, MA: Hendrickson, 2005.

Shelly, Rubel. "Baptism Does <u>Not</u> Sanctify an Adulterous Union." *Your Marriage Can Be Great.* Ed. Thomas B. Warren. Jonesboro, AR: National Christian Press, 1978. 551-556.

Spicq, Ceslas. *Theological Lexicon of the New Testament.* Peabody, MA: Hendrickson, 1994.

Sztanyo, Dick. "A Passage 'Requiring Them to Separate.'" *Your Marriage Can Be Great.* Ed. Thomas B. Warren. Jonesboro, AR: National Christian Press, 1978. 570-582.

Taylor, Robert R., Jr. "Crucial Questions Asked About Marriage." *Marriage, Divorce, and Remarriage (1992 Spiritual Sword Lectureship).* Ed. Jim Laws. Memphis, TN: Getwell, 1992. 54-73.

---. "Is It the Case That Alien Sinners Are Amenable to *Civil* Law Only, and Thus *Not* to the Law (Gospel) of Christ?" *The Spiritual Sword: Another Look at Marriage, Divorce, Remarriage.* 19:1 (1987): 3-6.

Varner, Terry. "It Is the Case That the Scriptures Teach That One Must Continue in Any Marriage That He Is in When Called Whether It Be His First, Second, Third, or Any Number." *The Spiritual Sword: Another Look at Marriage, Divorce, Remarriage.* 19:1 (1987): 26-28.

Vine, W.E. *Vine's Complete Expository Dictionary of Old and New Testament Words.* Nashville: Nelson, 1996.

Warren, Thomas B. "A General Look at Divorce & Remarriage." *The Spiritual Sword: Marriage, Divorce, Remarriage.* 6:2 (1975): 1-9.

---. "All Men—Including Non-Christians—Are Amenable to Christ's Law on Divorce and Remarriage." *Your Marriage Can Be Great.* Ed. Thomas B. Warren. Jonesboro, AR: National Christian Press, 1978. 361-368.

---. "Some More Crucial Questions Which Show the Distinction Between Truth and Error on Divorce and Remarriage." *Your Marriage Can Be Great.* Ed. Thomas B. Warren. Jonesboro, AR: National Christian Press, 1978. 387-402.

---. "There Is One—and Only One—Ground for Divorce and Remarriage." *Your Marriage Can Be Great.* Ed. Thomas B. Warren. Jonesboro, AR: National Christian Press, 1978. 356-360.

Winkler, Wendell. *Solving Problems God's Way.* Tuscaloosa, AL: Winkler Publications, 2004.

Woods, Guy N. "Answers to Some Questions on Divorce and Remarriage." *Your Marriage Can Be Great.* Ed. Thomas B. Warren. Jonesboro, AR: National Christian Press, 1978. 534-537.

Workman, Gary. "Key Scriptures: 1 Corinthians 7:1-40." *Marriage, Divorce, and Remarriage (1992 Spiritual Sword Lectureship).* Ed. Jim Laws. Memphis, TN: Getwell, 1992. 375-416.

OTHER SOURCES
(In addition to the bibliographies listed at the end of each chapter)

Connally, Andrew. *Connally-Hicks Debate.* Jonesboro, AR: National Christian Press, 1979.

Deaver, Mac. *Hicks-Deaver Debate.* Searcy, AR: Gospel Enterprises, 1995.

Deaver, Roy. *Marriage, Divorce and Remarriage.* 1977.

Duke, Kerry. *The Remarriage of a Divorced Couple.* Tompkinsville, KY: Duke, 1989.

Frost, Gene. *Dabney-Frost Debate.* 1959.

Frost, Gene. *Frost-Moyer Debate.*

Halbrook, Ron. *Halbrook-Freeman Debate.* Bowling Green, KY: Guardian of Truth, 1995.

Holt, Jack. *Hicks-Holt Debate.* Searcy, AR: Gospel Enterprises, 1990.

Lusk, Maurice W., III. *Marriage, Divorce and Remarriage.* Atlanta: Lusk, 1982.

Miller, Dave. *To Be or "Knot" To Be.* Pulaski, TN: Sain Publications, 1986.

Moffitt, Jerry. *Bales' Position Explained and Denied.* Austin, TX: Moffitt, 1982.

Music, Gosbel. *Divorce.* Colleyville, TX: Music, 1987.

Music, Goebel. *Separation Is Sin.* Colleyville, TX: Music, 1985.

Smith, J.T. *Smith-Lovelady Debate.* Brooks, KY: Search the Scriptures, 1976

Tarbet, Don. *Expose of Errors About Adultery.* Denison, TX: Tarbet, nd.

Tarbet, Don. *Tarbet-Edwards Debate.* San Antonio, TX: Thrust, nd.

Waldron, Jim E. *Hicks-Waldron Debate.* Harriman, TN: Waldron, 2007.

Warren, Thomas B. *Charts You Can Use in Preaching, Teaching and Studying on Divorce and Remarriage.* Jonesboro, AR: National Christian Press, 1978.

Warren, Thomas B. *Keeping the Lock in Wedlock.* Jonesboro, AR: National Christian Press, 1980.

Warren, Thomas B. *Under Bondage to the Law of Christ—The Only Real Freedom.* Moore, OK: National Christian Press, 1989.

Warren, Thomas B. *Warren-Fuqua Debate.* 1954.

Made in the USA
San Bernardino, CA
21 January 2018